Student Study Guide

to accompany

DYNAMICS *of* DEMOCRACY

Second Edition

PEVERILL SQUIRE
University of Iowa

JAMES M. LINDSAY
University of Iowa

CARY R. COVINGTON
University of Iowa

ERIC R.A.N. SMITH
University of California-Santa Barbara

Prepared by
BRIAN L. FIFE
Ball State University

Brown & Benchmark
PUBLISHERS

Madison, WI Dubuque   Guilford, CT   Chicago   Toronto London
Mexico City Caracas   Buenos Aires Madrid   Bogota Sydney

ISBN 0-697-32767-1

Printed in the United States of America

10 9 8 7 6 5 4 3 2 1

Contents

Preface iv

1   Studying the Dynamics of Democracy: Conflict, Rules, and Change   1

2   Constitution   7

3   The Social Context of American Politics   19

4   Civil Liberties   25

5   Civil Rights   32

6   Public Opinion   41

7   Voting and Participation   50

8   The News Media   58

9   Political Parties   66

10   Interest Groups   74

11   Congress   82

12   The Presidency   92

13   The Federal Bureaucracy   101

14   The Courts   109

15   The Federal System and State Government   117

16   The Federal Budget   125

17   Domestic Policy   133

18   Foreign Policy   141

Preface

This study guide has been prepared to help you, the student, understand the facts behind the organization of American government as well as its basic principles and conflicting ideals. It is designed to be used with *The Dynamics of Democracy*, 2nd edition. In order to be an effective learning tool, each chapter of this study guide contains the following items:

SUMMARY: This is a brief introduction to the material covered in the chapter.

OUTLINE: This is an outline of the material in the chapter, including the major headings of each chapter along with page references.

KEY TERMS, CONCEPTS, EVENTS, AND PEOPLE: This extensive list includes not only glossary terms defined in the text, but also concepts, events, and important people along with the page numbers on which they are discussed. You might find it useful for reviewing material to jot down a brief definition next to each item, or to use the list when studying with a friend to quiz each other on the items.

LEARNING OBJECTIVES: These are the basic concepts discussed in the chapter.

PRACTICE TEST: This section of the study guide gives you an opportunity to test your knowledge of the material in the chapter. This section will help you study for tests and exams. It consists of three sections: *Multiple Choice Questions*, *Short Essay Questions*, and *Critical Thinking Exercises*. The Short Essay section asks you to respond to an idea or a concept in more depth than you would an objective question. The Critical Thinking Exercises challenge you to apply chapter concepts to real-world events.

ANSWERS: Each chapter provides the answers to its practice test items. The Short Essay answer, while brief, still gives you the basis for an answer. You may want to check the text for a more elaborate response.

A FINAL NOTE

Please note that the spaces provided to fill in answers are estimates of the space you may need. We have made every effort to provide the correct amount of space for an average style of handwriting, but you may need more or less. In any case, this study guide, if used diligently, should provide you with an effective tool for learning about your American government and the politics behind it.

SUMMARY

The theme of the book is delineated in this chapter by the authors. All political systems, including the democratic government in the United States, are rooted in conflict. Conflict is an inherent feature of all societies because of material scarcity and disagreements over values. As a result, the diverse activities that constitute politics all have one factor in common—people are motivated by conflict. The federal government has the primary task for managing conflict in society. In order for a government to succeed at managing conflict, it needs to possess both legitimacy and coercive force.

OUTLINE

Opening Story: Contract with America and Term Limits

In the 1994 congressional elections, Republican candidates for the House of Representatives committed themselves to a campaign platform known as the Contract with America. One of the provisions in the Contract was a constitutional proposal for term limits, which would limit the number of terms anyone could serve in the House or the Senate. According to Republican proponents, Congress had strayed away from the Framers' vision of a "citizen legislature" and had become an institution dominated by professional politicians. The concept of term limits enjoyed a great deal of support among the American people. Yet in spite of the widespread support for term limits and the fact that the Republicans took control of both chambers as a result of the 1994 elections, term limits have failed to become part of the U.S. Constitution. Inherent in any political system is conflict. Once the Republicans commenced debating the issue in the House, it became clear that there were differences in opinion over the length and scope of term limits. Furthermore, many senior Republicans in the House dismissed term limits as a bad idea. A large majority of Democrats opposed term limits. The Republican leaders did succeed in bringing four different term limits bills to the floor for a vote. After a great deal of tumultuous debate, all proposals were defeated. In order to amend the Constitution, a two-thirds majority vote is needed in both the House and the Senate. If this is achieved, three-fourths of the state legislatures (38 states) must vote to ratify the proposal. The term limits movement in the House fell far short of the two-thirds requirement.

Politics and Conflict (p. 8)

The Roots of Conflict (p. 8)

The Role of Government in Managing Conflict (p. 9)

Government as Rule Maker (p. 11)

Structural Rules (p. 11)

Policy Rules (p. 12)

The Biased Character of Rules (p. 14)

The Changing Rules of Government (p. 15)

Putting It All Together: Context, Participants, Institutions, and Processes (p. 16)

The Context of American Politics (p. 16)

Individuals and Groups in American Politics (p. 16)

The Institutions of American Politics (p. 17)

The Policy Process in American Politics (p. 17)

Summary (p. 18)

Key Terms (p. 18)

Readings for Further Study (p. 18)

KEY TERMS, CONCEPTS, EVENTS, AND PEOPLE

Be able to identify and/or define each of the following and state its importance in a short paragraph.

Contract with America (p. 4)

Term limits (p. 4)

Material scarcity (p. 8)

Legitimacy (p. 10)

Coercive force (p. 10)

Structural rules (p. 11)

Policy rule (p. 12)

Context of American Politics (p. 16)

Individuals and Groups in American Politics (p. 16)

Institutions of American Politics (p. 17)

Policy Process in American Politics (p. 17)

LEARNING OBJECTIVES

After reading chapter 1, students should be able to:

1. Explain and give concrete examples of how politics involves conflicts among different groups in a society.
2. Explain how the rules used to manage political conflicts affect who wins and who loses in particular conflicts.
3. Identify material scarcity and disagreements over basic values and beliefs as the two main sources of political conflict in a society.
4. Explain why political conflict is inherent to any society.
5. Identify government as the social institution charged with managing a society's internal political conflicts.
6. Define the concepts of legitimacy and coercive force, and explain why each is important to a government's success in managing political conflict.
7. Identify "consent of the governed" as the basis for government legitimacy in the United States.
8. Distinguish between and give examples of structural policy rules.
9. Give examples of the inherent bias of all government rules, (structural and policy), while distinguishing between bias and fairness in rules.
10. Defend the claim that government rules (structural and policy) in the United States have changed repeatedly through history, and be able to give concrete examples of government rules that have changed.

PRACTICE EXAM

(Answers appear at the end of this chapter)

Multiple Choice

1. Which of the following House Republicans was a vocal opponent of term limits in 1995?
   a. Henry Hyde
   b. Newt Gingrich
   c. Richard Armey
   d. Bob Inglis

2. What did the Supreme Court rule on state laws limiting service in the U.S. Congress?
   a. Nothing.
   b. The justices ruled that such laws were constitutional.
   c. The justices ruled that such laws were unconstitutional.
   d. The justices called for a constitutional convention to settle the term limits dispute.

3. What does the fight over term limits illustrate?
   a. Politics arises from conflict.
   b. The rules of government help determine who wins political battles.
   c. Both a and b.
   d. Public opinion is the decisive factor in all congressional debates.

4. People who participate in politics are all motivated by
   a. conflict.
   b. greed.
   c. the desire to serve the greater public interest.
   d. the desire to become a powerful politician.

5. Conflict is an inherent feature of all societies because
   a. of the existence of material scarcity.
   b. people disagree over core values.
   c. there are rich and poor people.
   d. All of the above.

6. Which of the following is the ultimate authority in the U.S.?
   a. President
   b. Internal Revenue Service
   c. Congress
   d. The people

7. To succeed at managing conflict, what does a government need?
   a. A strong army
   b. A popular leader
   c. Legitimacy and coercive force
   d. Favorable public opinion ratings as well as low taxes

8. Where do we find the most important structural rules in the U.S.?
   a. The Declaration of Independence
   b. The U.S. Constitution
   c. Laws passed by the Congress
   d. Rulings handed down by the Supreme Court

9. Which of the following is an example of a policy rule?
   a. The president is elected by the Electoral College
   b. Members of the U.S. Senate have a six year term
   c. Earnings will be taxed at the rate of 28%
   d. Women can vote in elections

10. Rules create
    a. winners and losers.
    b. equality for all.
    c. a society with little or no conflict.
    d. fair representation in the U.S. Congress.

Essays

11. Why is conflict an inherent feature in all societies, whether it be Haiti, Rwanda, North Korea, Great Britain, the United States, or any country?
12. Since conflict is a problem in all countries, what prevent it from escalating into political violence and civil war?
13. How does a government manage conflict, and how does it make choices about how society will operate?
14. Are governmental rules neutral in their effect? Explain.

15. Have governmental rules in the United States changed very much over the last two hundred years? Explain.

CRITICAL THINKING EXERCISES

1. Select one of the following conflictual issues and explain how the U.S. government has managed it in recent years. Feel free to consult external references in this exercise.
   a. Capital Punishment
   b. Abortion
   c. Gun Control
   d. Flag Burning
2. Material scarcity exists in all countries, even in a country as wealthy as the United States. Go to your library and find out how income levels differ across America. A good source to consult is *The Statistical Abstract of the United States.*

ANSWERS TO THE PRACTICE EXAM

1. A
2. C
3. C
4. A
5. D
6. D
7. C
8. B
9. C
10. A

11. Conflict is an inherent feature of all societies because it stems from two things that can never change: material scarcity and differences in values. Material scarcity means that no country can provide its people with everything they need or desire. This is true in the poorest of nations as well as in the United States. Because no government can meet all the physical needs and wants of all its citizens, conflict is inevitable because different groups compete over who should get how much of what is available in the country. The second reason political conflict is inevitable is that no country in history has produced a society in which all of its members had the same values, principles, and beliefs. People disagree over the kind of society they want for themselves and others and conflict arises.

12. The government prevents conflict from escalating into violence and civil war, for the simple reason that the government is the only institution in a country that has the requisite authority to manage conflict. The authority of a government stems from its legitimacy (the willingness of citizens to obey governmental decisions) and with its ability to control the use of coercive force in society (forcing citizens to comply with governmental decisions).

13. A government manages conflict by devising rules that structure how political decisions will be made and then by issuing rules that determine the winners and losers on specific policy issues. Structural rules establish the organization, structure, and powers of government, and can be found in the United States primarily in the Constitution. A policy rule is established when a government institution makes a decision on a particular issue, such as the funding for various social programs.

14. Rules devised by governments are not neutral in their effect. Rules always create winners and losers, because they advance the interests of some parties and restrict the interests of others. Both structural and policy rules are inherently biased. The biased nature of structural rules is witnessed in the composition of the U.S. Senate. The Constitution stipulates that all states, regardless of their population, will have two senators. This means that a large state such as California has the same representation as a small state such as Wyoming. Perhaps even more straightforward, policy rules are often the subject of vocal debates. Different rules benefit different groups in society, and that is why groups compete with a great deal of intensity over policy making.

15. The rules of the American government have changed a great deal in its history. Structural rules concerning who can vote have been altered considerably. Today, virtually all citizens over the age of eighteen can vote. After the Constitution was ratified, only white males over the age of twenty-one could vote. Women could not vote, and neither could men of color. Policy rules have also evolved over time, to such a great extent that change is truly the one constant in American politics.

Chapter **2** **Constitution**

SUMMARY

The Constitution was written in 1787 because the confederal government created under the Articles of Confederation was a failure. From May to September, the framers had to contend with conflicting political ambitions and objectives. They were also influenced by their political philosophies. Their ultimate concern was to protect individual rights. In order to preserve fundamental rights, the framers opted to create a republican form of government in which citizens would elect representatives to govern on their behalf. In this new federal form of government, power was shared between the national government and the states.

OUTLINE

Opening Story: The "Republican Revolution" of 1995

Even though the Constitution was written in 1787, it still provides the basic structural rules of American politics. Regardless of time period, in order to understand American government, students need to familiarize themselves with the Constitution, the rules it sets forth, and how those rules are interpreted in practice. Upon doing so, it is easier to understand why the Republicans failed to enact revolutionary changes in 1995, despite the historic 1994 congressional elections where they took control of both chambers in the legislative branch for the first time in forty years.

After the 1994 elections, the Republicans, and particularly the House Republicans, believed that they had a mandate to make revolutionary changes in public policy. But by the end of the year, only one of the Contract with America provisions had been enacted. Relatively few other Republican proposals had become law as well. So why, therefore, was the "Republican Revolution" not more successful? One only needs to examine the U.S. Constitution, the supreme law of the land, to understand why the Republicans did not meet with more success in their legislative agenda.

The rules set forth in the Constitution were designed to prevent intense majorities from making drastic changes in public policy. The Constitution requires both houses of Congress to approve all bills. Many Republican senators did not agree with their House counterparts on key provisions of the Contract with America, so they ignored, watered down, and rejected many bills passed in the House. Similarly, the Constitution gives veto power to the president, to strike down legislation of which he/she does not approve. President Bill Clinton made frequent use of this power, and the Republicans lacked the votes to override him (a two-thirds vote in each chamber is required to override a presidential veto). Thus, the limited success of the "Republican Revolution" in 1995 reminds us all that the U.S. is a nation of laws where the most fundamental are set forth in the Constitution.

The Constitution as a Reflection of Political Conflict (p. 20)

The Colonial Experience (p. 21)

The Articles of Confederation (p. 22)

The Politics of the Constitutional Convention (p. 23)

The Politics of Ratification (p. 28)

The Constitution as a Reflection of the Founders' Philosophy (p. 31)

Individual Rights and Democratic Rule (p. 32)

Majority Tyranny: The Paradox of Majority Rule (p. 32)

Preventing Majority Tyranny (p. 33)

The Core Provisions of the Constitution (p. 38)

Congress (p. 38)

The Presidency and the Executive Branch (p. 39)

The Federal Judiciary (p. 40)

Interstate Relations (p. 41)

Other Provisions (p. 42)

Three Consequences of the Constitution (p. 42)

The Protection of Individual Rights (p .42)

A Bias in Favor of the Status Quo (p. 43)

Political Flexibility (p. 44)

Federalism: The Vertical Dimension to the Constitution (p. 46)

Confederal, Unitary, and Federal Governments (p. 47)

Establishing National Supremacy (p. 47)

The Assertion of States' Rights (p. 49)

The Civil War and the Reassertion of National Supremacy (p. 50)

Dual Federalism (p. 51)

The Present Era—National Supremacy as Fiscal Federalism (p. 51)

Summary (p. 53)

Key Terms (p. 54)

Readings for Further Study (p. 54)

The Constitution of the United States (p. 55)

KEY TERMS, CONCEPTS, EVENTS, AND PEOPLE

Be able to identify and/or define each of the following and state its importance in a short paragraph.

"No taxation without representation" (p. 21)

Articles of Confederation (p. 22)

Confederal government (p. 22)

Shays's Rebellion (p. 23)

Virginia Plan (p. 24)

New Jersey Plan (p. 25)

Connecticut Compromise (p. 26)

Three-fifths Compromise (p. 26)

Federalists (p. 28)

Patrick Henry (p. 28)

James Madison (p. 29)

Antifederalists (p. 29)

Bill of Rights (p. 30)

Classical liberalism (p. 32)

John Locke (p. 32)

Majority tyranny (p. 32)

Federalist Papers (p. 33)

Democracy (p. 34)

Republicanism (p. 34)

Separation of Powers (p. 35)

Checks and Balances (p. 35)

Bicameral legislature (p. 36)

Concurrent majorities (p. 36)

Supermajority (p. 36)

Federalism (p. 37)

Habeas Corpus (p. 37)

Bills of Attainder (p. 37)

Ex post facto laws (p. 37)

Necessary and Proper Clause (p. 39)

McCulloch v. Maryland (p. 39)

Establishment clause (p. 43)

Unitary government (p. 47)

John Marshall (p. 48)

Roger Taney (p. 48)

National Supremacy (p. 48)

States' Rights (p. 49)

Doctrine of interposition (p. 49)

Doctrine of nullification (p. 49)

Dred Scott Case (p. 49)

Dual federalism (p. 51)

Fiscal federalism (p. 51)

Great Depression (p. 52)

New Deal (p. 52)

Great Society (p. 52)

Interstate commerce clause (p. 52)

LEARNING OBJECTIVES

After reading chapter 2, students should be able to:

1. Explain how the founders' experiences with colonial rule and the Articles of Confederation shaped their views of how much power should be vested in the national government and the executive office.
2. Describe the differences between the Virginia and New Jersey Plans and explain how the Connecticut Compromise resolved that conflict.
3. Explain why slavery was an explosive issue at the Constitutional Convention and show how the three-fifths rule enabled the founders to agree on a way to deal with the issue of slavery.
4. Explain why the Constitution only vaguely defines the powers of the president and identify the political consequences of that ambiguity.
5. Explain why the Antifederalists opposed the Constitution.
6. Explain how the rules for ratifying the Constitution gave the Federalists an advantage over the Antifederalists.
7. Describe why the Federalists agreed to support the amendments to the Constitution known as the Bill of Rights.
8. Describe classical liberalism and explain why it supports the creation of democratic governments that use majority rule to make decisions.
9. Explain why making decisions on the basis of majority rule creates the potential paradox of majority tyranny.
10. Show how the Constitution's rule for electing members of Congress and the president help deter the formation of permanent majorities.
11. Explain the difference between separation of powers and checks and balances, and show how they deter majority tyranny.
12. Identify the differences between simple, concurrent and supermajority voting rules and explain how the latter two protect minorities.
13. Identify provisions in the Constitution and Bill of Rights that place formal limits on the boundaries of government action.
14. Identify three important ways in which the Constitution affects the way American government works.
15. Explain the different ways in which unitary, federal, and confederal forms of government allocate sovereignty between levels of government.
16. Explain how and why the meaning of federalism has changed over the course of American history.
17. Explain why the United States adopted the doctrine of fiscal federalism and discuss how it differs from dual federalism.

PRACTICE EXAM

(Answers appear at the end of this chapter)

Multiple Choice

1. Why did King George III decide to exert more control over the colonies in the middle of the eighteenth century?
   a. He grew tired of the radical colonists.
   b. He wanted to punish the colonists for dumping tea in Boston Harbor.
   c. He needed revenue to pay the costs of the French and Indian War.
   d. He wanted revenue to expand his palace.

2. Why was the American Revolutionary War fought?
   a. The colonists wanted to preserve the liberties that they already enjoyed.
   b. The colonists wanted to obtain freedom from Great Britain.
   c. The colonists wanted Samuel Adams to be their leader.
   d. The colonists wanted a republican form of government.

3. The Articles of Confederation was written in
   a. 1763.
   b. 1776.
   c. 1777.
   d. 1789.

4. The Articles of Confederation created a
   a. powerful national government.
   b. national government consisting of one branch--the executive branch.
   c. national government consisting of two branches--the legislative and judicial branches.
   d. Congress that could not regulate interstate commerce.

5. Shays's Rebellion demonstrated that
   a. Congress could govern effectively in periods of crises.
   b. Congress could not govern effectively in periods of crises.
   c. state governments could always rely on the national government to assist them in dealing with armed rebellions.
   d. the president would help state governors with violence within their borders.

6. The Constitution was written in
   a. 1777.
   b. 1787.
   c. 1791.
   d. 1795.

7. Under the Virginia Plan,
   a. every voter in the United States would be represented equally in the national legislature.
   b. every state in the United States would be represented equally in the national legislature.
   c. slavery would be abolished.
   d. the less populous states would have as much political power as Massachusetts, Pennsylvania, and Virginia.

8. In the three-fifths compromise, the debate over slavery became intertwined with the debate over
   a. the natural rights of black Americans.
   b. federalism.
   c. state boundaries.
   d. representation in the U.S. House of Representatives.

9. _____ was a vocal Federalist.
   a. Thomas Jefferson
   b. Alexander Hamilton
   c. Patrick Henry
   d. Samuel Adams

10. Classical liberalism emphasizes
    a. the rights of individuals.
    b. using the federal government to solve problems in society.
    c. using state governments to solve problems in society.
    d. None of the above.

11. Which individuals wrote the *Federalist Papers?*
    a. George Washington, Alexander Hamilton, John Marshall.
    b. Thomas Jefferson, James Madison, Aaron Burr.
    c. James Madison, Alexander Hamilton, John Jay.
    d. James Madison, Benjamin Franklin, Gouverneur Morris.

12. Article I of the Constitution created the _____ branch of government, reflecting the founders' belief that it should be the dominant branch of government.
    a. executive
    b. judicial
    c. legislative
    d. administrative

13. Who authored the 27th amendment (1992), which stipulated that a sitting Congress could not raise its own salary?
    a. George Bush
    b. George Mitchell
    c. Tom Foley
    d. James Madison

14. The most common mode of amending the Constitution is by a
    a. simple majority vote in Congress, and a 2/3 ratification vote in the state legislatures.
    b. 3/4 vote in Congress, and a 3/4 vote in the state legislatures.
    c. 2/3 vote in Congress, and a 3/4 vote in the state conventions.
    d. 2/3 vote in Congress, and a 3/4 vote in the state legislatures.

15. Which of the following is an example of a confederal form of government?
    a. Great Britain
    b. United Nations
    c. North Korea
    d. Scotland

16. What was the factual basis of *McCulloch v. Maryland?*
    a. Does Congress have the power to regulate interstate commerce?
    b. Does Congress have the power to tax personal income?
    c. Does Congress have the power to create a national bank?
    d. Does Congress have the power to build lighthouses?

17. Chief Justices John Marshall and Roger Taney disagreed on the meaning of
    a. federalism.
    b. the roles of the national and state governments.
    c. states' rights.
    d. All of the above.

18. What metaphor can be used to describe dual federalism?
    a. layer cake
    b. marble cake
    c. German chocolate cake
    d. Texas sheet cake

19. The shift from dual to fiscal federalism was triggered by
    a. the Civil War.
    b. the Dred Scott decision.
    c. the Great Depression.
    d. World War II.

20. When tracing the meaning of federalism in the U.S., the Constitution can be described as
    a. a rigid document.
    b. a flexible document.
    c. a failed document.
    d. None of the above.

Essays

21. What was the conflict between the Federalists and the Antifederalists? How was it resolved?
22. What steps did the Framers take to prevent the emergence of a permanent majority that would suppress the rights of the minority? Explain.
23. Explain how power is divvied up amongst the three branches of government in Articles I, II, and III of the Constitution. Be sure to include concrete examples of checks and balances and separation of powers.

24. The principles and rules of the Constitution have had a significant effect on politics in the United States. What are the three most important consequences of the Constitution?
25. Describe the current era of federalism in the United States.

CRITICAL THINKING EXERCISES

1. Some are critical of the Framers for the manner in which they contended with, or failed to contend with, the issue of slavery. What are your thoughts on this source of conflict for the architects of the Constitution?
2. The Electoral College was created at the Philadelphia Convention as a compromise between those who wanted Congress to select the president and those who wanted direct election of eligible voters. Is the Electoral College still a good mechanism for electing a president? Why or why not? Try to come up with five reasons to support your contention.
3. Assume that the Southern confederacy defeated the Union forces in the Civil War. How would the nature of federalism have been different as a result? How would the United States be different today?

ANSWERS TO THE PRACTICE EXAM

1.	C	11.	C
2.	A	12.	C
3.	C	13.	D
4.	D	14.	D
5.	B	15.	B
6.	B	16.	C
7.	A	17.	D
8.	D	18.	A
9.	B	19.	C
10.	A	20.	B

21. The Federalists supported ratification of the Constitution and the Antifederalists opposed it. Federalists believed that the Constitution was needed to remedy the problems experienced under the Articles of Confederation. Antifederalists feared that the Constitution gave too much power to the national government, and that it would infringe on the rights of state governments and individuals. The conflict was addressed when the Federalists promised to amend the Constitution to include a list of provisions guaranteeing certain individual rights (the list later became known as the Bill of Rights).

22. The Framers took three important steps to prevent the emergence of a permanent majority that would suppress the rights of the minority. First, they organized elections in a manner that would make it difficult for permanent electoral majorities to form. Second, they divided authority among government institutions at the national level as well as between the federal government and the state governments. Third, they placed formal boundaries on what the government may do. Each of these steps created a barrier to majority tyranny. The Framers clearly placed a high value on preventing government from making decisions that would suppress the rights of the minority.

23. [Students need to carefully read and study Articles I, II, and III to provide a cogent response to this question].

24. The three most important consequences of the Constitution involve the following: the protection of individual rights, a bias in favor of the status quo, and political flexibility. Today, all levels of government are limited in their ability to pass laws that infringe on individual rights. A concrete illustration of this involves the conflict over school prayer. A strong majority of Americans favor prayer in the public schools, yet the Supreme Court has invalidated this practice due to the First Amendment. A second consequence concerns the preservation of

the status quo. Before any bill becomes a law, there has to be a high level of consensus between the House of Representatives, the Senate, and the president. As a result, and sometimes regardless of merit, most bills never become law in the United States. Even when a majority favors change, as was witnessed in the struggle for the ERA to become part of the Constitution, the rules established by the Framers make it difficult to happen. A final important consequence of the Constitution is that it is sufficiently flexible to meet the country's changing needs. In spite of the bias to preserve the status quo, the Constitution has weathered the times because of the amending process, its ambiguity, and its relative silence on many political aspects of government. Much of the Constitution is written in general language, which has allowed the government to adapt more easily to societal changes and to the expectations of the public.

25. In the 1930s, a new interpretation of federalism evolved which still continues today. Under this new version, federal laws were not only superior to state laws, but the federal government also had the responsibility for providing financial assistance to the states. This newest form of federalism is called fiscal federalism. The shift from dual to fiscal federalism began as a result of the Great Depression. The states were unable to revive the stagnant economy and contend with a host of social policy issues, so President Franklin Delano Roosevelt responded by making the federal government a provider of services to states and to individuals. Unlike past times when their relationships were more conflictual, the states have accepted federal pre-eminence in exchange for much needed financial resources.

Chapter 3

The Social Context of American Politics

SUMMARY

American society has changed vastly since the Constitution was written. Once a largely agrarian society, the United States is now predominantly urban. The population is one of the most diverse in the world, and it has risen to over 260 million residents. Often thought of as a melting pot, this image is erroneous because many Americans maintain their sense of racial or ethnic identity. The changing social composition has given rise to many potential sources of conflict yet, fortunately, the tremendous diversity of American society is also a strength which precludes the government from catering to the interests of one elite group. The authors argue that the American political system can be characterized as being pluralistic—meaning that on different issues, different groups tend to exercise power. Though pluralists reject the assertion that a single elite wields power in the United States, they do recognize that Americans do not share political or economic power equally.

OUTLINE

Opening Story: Understanding American Society

The results of surveys indicate that many Americans do not understand the racial and ethnic makeup of their society. The average American believes that over half of the population is nonwhite, when in reality whites constitute about 75% of the population.

Understanding what the country looks like is important because the American government is supposed to be representative of all people. How Americans identify themselves determines how they view their political, social, and economic interests. In turn, this shapes the demands they make on government and the kind of political rules they favor.

Conflict has been largely avoided in the United States, in spite of the heterogeneous population. The political system has been successful at managing conflict because there is a lot of overlap between the groups in society and because it is pluralistic (i.e., responsive to many groups).

Who Are Americans? (p. 68)

A Growing and Changing Population (p. 69)

Race and Ethnicity (p. 72)

Immigration (p. 76)

Language (p. 77)

Age (p. 78)

Family Households (p. 78)

Sexual Orientation (p. 79)

Social and Economic Characteristics (p. 80)

Religion (p. 80)

Education (p. 81)

Wealth and Income (p. 82)

Home Ownership (p. 86)

Occupation (p. 86)

Diversity and Social Harmony (p. 88)

Political Power in the United States (p. 89)

Summary (p. 91)

Key Terms (p. 92)

Readings for Further Study (p. 92)

KEY TERMS, CONCEPTS, EVENTS, AND PEOPLE

Be able to identify and/or define each of the following and state its importance in a short paragraph.

Sun Belt states (p. 72)

Rust Belt states (p. 72)

Baby boomers (p. 78)

Feminization of poverty (p. 86)

Cross-cutting cleavages (p. 88)

Pluralism (p. 90)

Power (p. 90)

LEARNING OBJECTIVES

After reading chapter 3, students should be able to:

1. Discuss how the size of the American population has grown enormously since the founding of the nation and show how the demographic and social makeup of the American population has changed.
2. Describe racial and ethnic makeup of the United States and to show that Hispanic Americans and Asian Americans have a faster growth rate than other racial or ethnic groups.
3. Explain how the United States is a multicultural society and what multiculturalism is likely to mean for America in the future.
4. Describe immigration patterns in the United States and how issues surrounding legal and illegal immigration differ.
5. Defend the claim that while English is the dominant language in the United States, many Americans speak another language at home, and to explain that recent immigrants both want to and are learning English just as their predecessors did.
6. Describe how the average age in the United States has increased substantially over the past two hundred years and to explain what impact the increasing number of elderly people has on the American political system.
7. Explain that while most Americans still live in families, the average family size is decreasing and the number of people living in single-parent households is increasing.
8. Describe the debate over the number of gays and lesbians living in the United States and to explain why the outcome of this debate has important political consequences.
9. Show that most Americans are religious, but that they are divided among a large number of religious denominations.
10. Describe how the average level of education in the United States has increased over the course of the twentieth century and explain how educational achievement varies by race and sex.
11. Describe the distribution of wealth and income in the United States and to show how it is strongly linked to race and education.
12. Explain how most Americans live in homes they own and discuss how home ownership is less common among African Americans and Hispanic Americans than among the white majority.
13. Discuss the enormous changes wrought by the enormous changes in what most Americans do for a living as the economy evolved from farming to manufacturing and more recently to service industry.
14. Explain how America's diversity is a source of potential conflict and explain how cross-cutting cleavages dampen the conflict and make it manageable.
15. Explain the concept of pluralism and show how it applies to politics in the United States.

PRACTICE EXAM

(Answers appear at the end of this chapter)

Multiple Choice

1. According to the U.S. Census Bureau, _____ % of Americans identify themselves as white.
   a. 35
   b. 50
   c. 60
   d. 75

2. According to the U.S. Census Bureau, _____ % of Americans identify themselves as black.
   a. 5
   b. 12
   c. 22
   d. 35

3. According to the U.S. Census Bureau, what is the approximate population in the United States?
   a. 150 million
   b. 200 million
   c. 265 million
   d. 300 million

4. How has the population changed since 1900?
   a. It has gotten older.
   b. The average American is a homeowner.
   c. Women outnumber men.
   d. All of the above.

5. Which ethnic group is the largest in the United States?
   a. Northern Europeans
   b. African Americans
   c. Hispanic Americans
   d. Asian Americans

6. What is the largest religious denomination in the United States?
   a. Baptists
   b. Roman Catholics
   c. Lutherans
   d. Jews

7. Income in the United States is strongly linked to _____ and _____.
   a. ideology, motivation
   b. hobbies, marital status
   c. race, education
   d. religion, education

8. Which of the following does NOT represent a dramatic change in the American economic landscape?
   a. The economy has shifted from a manufacturing to a service economy.
   b. Almost half the population makes a living by farming the land.
   c. The number of union workers is declining.
   d. Over 60% of all married women work outside the home.

9. In Floyd Hunter's study of Atlanta, he concluded that
   a. public policy making was dominated by a power elite.
   b. public policy making was the product of diverse competition between interest groups.
   c. public policy making was the product of the news media.
   d. None of the above.

10. In Robert Dahl's study of New Haven, he concluded that
    a. public policy making was dominated by a power elite.
    b. public policy making was pluralistic.
    c. business leaders controlled most public policy issues.
    d. None of the above.

Essays

11. How is American society different than when George Washington was president? What effect has this change had on the political system?
12. Explain what is meant by the melting pot theory. Why is it misleading?
13. Why is there very little class conflict in the United States?
14. Many characterizations of poverty suggest that it is a problem largely facing minorities in the U.S. Is this accurate? Why or why not?
15. How do the authors describe political power in the U.S.?

CRITICAL THINKING EXERCISES

1. Find out the racial balance of the student population at your college or university. What implications does it have for policy making at your institution?
2. Go to a town/city meeting in your hometown. How does politics work in your area? Is it more like Hunter's elitism or Dahl's pluralism? Explain.

ANSWERS TO THE PRACTICE EXAM

1.   D
2.   B
3.   C
4.   D
5.   A
6.   B
7.   C
8.   B
9.   A
10. B

11. When George Washington became the first president of the United States, the population was less than 4 million people. Today, the population is approximately 265 million. He presided over the 13 original colonies; now there are 50 states. In 1795, there were 4.5 people per square mile, and in 1990 there were 74.6. A growing population places more demands on government and more problems for it to solve. The dramatic increase in population has been accompanied by equally dramatic changes in where Americans live. In Washington's era, America was largely a society of small farmers. Historically, the U.S. has moved from a rural to an urban society. Yet in recent decades, more people have moved to the suburbs, than in central cities or rural areas. As the U.S. population becomes more suburban, the interests of both inner-city dwellers and ruralites have become secondary. This is due to the fact that legislators are most responsive to the group in society that commands the most votes. Finally, the population was based in the Eastern United States in 1790; at the present time, the fastest growing region is the Sun Belt. This means that people in the Rust Belt have been given less attention by the government.

12. Most Americans think of the United States as a melting pot of people from many different backgrounds. According to this theory, regardless of race or ethnicity, all Americans assimilate as one, as if they were put into a huge pot and came out as a generic American. This is misleading, however. The reality is that many Americans have maintained their own sense of racial or ethnic identity. With an increasingly heterogeneous population, this has important implications for politics.

23

13.   In many countries politics is organized around class conflict. Indeed, many critics of capitalism contend that the upper class benefits by exploiting the labor of the working class. Yet class has rarely been a seriously divisive issue in the U.S. Despite evidence of the existence of lower, middle, and upper classes, most Americans do not think in class terms. In some surveys, an overwhelming majority of Americans identified themselves as middle class. As a result, politicians tend not to play off class distinctions because there would be little, or no, political reward for doing so.

14.   Poverty is a problem that affects all Americans. While black Americans and Hispanic Americans are about three times more likely than whites to live in poverty, more poor people are white than any other group. Whites constitute the largest group of poor Americans because they are by far the largest group in the country. In addition to this, poverty is not limited to the inner cities, but is also found in rural areas and even in the suburbs. Thus, characterizations of poverty as a problem facing minorities are very inaccurate.

15.   According to the authors, pluralism characterizes the American political system best. On different issues, different groups tend to exercise power. They examine two landmark studies of power in American cities—Hunter's investigation of Atlanta, and Dahl's examination of political power in New Haven, Connecticut. Hunter's study was flawed because he assumed that a power elite existed, but never demonstrated how this group influenced city government. Dahl found no single power elite in New Haven. Different groups exerted power on different issues, and he found that the city's business leaders exercised power on only a few issues. Dahl's findings were consistent with the theory of pluralism. Although pluralism rejects the contention that a single elite group wields power in the U.S., it recognizes that Americans do not share political or economic power equally.

SUMMARY

The fundamental rules governing the relationship between individuals and the government are set forth in the Constitution. Civil liberties are areas of personal freedom in which the government cannot interfere, and are largely rooted in the Bill of Rights. No liberties, however, are absolute. Throughout American history, the rights of the individual have been weighed against the rights of society. The meaning of the Constitution, as stipulated by the Supreme Court, is not fixed. Over the years the justices have interpreted the Constitution differently, depending upon the Court's membership. Throughout the history of the U.S., Americans have struggled to find a fair balance between the rights of the individual and the rights of society. This is undoubtedly destined to continue for some time.

OUTLINE

Opening Story: Rosenberger v. University of Virginia

In 1991, the editors of *Wide Awake,* a magazine designed to provide a "Christian perspective on both personal and community issues," at the University of Virginia were denied by administrative officials of their request for a university subsidy. University officials claimed that as a state agency, funding for religious groups violated the constitutional separation of church and state. The editors challenged the university's decision in federal court. The federal district court upheld the university's position, and the court of appeals affirmed. The Supreme Court, by a five-to-four margin, overturned these decisions and sided with the students.

In *Rosenberger v. University of Virginia,* the justices treated student religious magazines as if they were any other student publication, arguing that to do otherwise would risk suppressing free speech. The issues raised in this case are as old as the republic itself. Disagreements frequently have arise over how to interpret the structural rules of American politics, and many of these have led to bitter political conflict.

Interpreting the Constitution (p. 94)

The Bill of Rights and State Government (p. 96)

The First Amendment: Freedom of Speech, Assembly, Press, and Religion (p. 97)

Freedom of Speech (p. 97)

Freedom of Assembly and Association (p. 104)

Freedom of the Press (p. 105)

Freedom of Religion (p. 108)

The Second Amendment: The Right to Bear Arms? (p. 112)

State Militias (p. 113)

Supreme Court Rulings (p. 113)

Gun Control Laws (p. 115)

Government and the Rights of Criminal Suspects (p. 116)

The Fourth Amendment: Search and Seizure (p. 117)

The Fifth Amendment: Criminal Procedure for a Person Accused (p. 118)

The Sixth Amendment: Procedures for a People Charged with a Crime (p. 119)

The Eighth Amendment: Cruel and Unusual Punishment (p. 120)

Privacy as a Constitutional Right (p. 121)

Summary (p. 123)

Key Terms (p. 124)

Readings for Further Study (p. 124)

KEY TERMS, CONCEPTS, EVENTS, AND PEOPLE

Be able to identify and/or define each of the following and state its importance in a short paragraph.

Civil liberties (p. 94)

Original intent (p. 95)

Clear and present danger standard (p. 99)

Bad tendency doctrine (p. 100)

Incitement standard (p. 101)

Prior restraint (p. 105)

Pentagon Papers (p. 105)

Libel law (p. 106)

Obscenity law (p. 108)

Establishment clause (p. 108)

Free exercise clause (p. 108)

Exclusionary rule (p. 117)

Miranda rights (p. 119)

Roe v. Wade (p. 121)

LEARNING OBJECTIVES

After reading chapter 4, students should be able to:

1. Explain the difference between civil liberties and civil rights.
2. Analyze the limitations inherent in using original intent to interpret the meaning of the Constitution and to discuss how interpretations of the Constitution have changed over time.
3. Explain how the Supreme Court has changed its interpretation of freedom of speech over the past two centuries and to discuss the legal standards that prevail today for both political and symbolic speech.
4. Explain what the Constitution means when it says that the people have the right "peaceably to assemble, and to petition the Government for the redress of grievances."
5. Discuss how freedom of the press has evolved over the years and to explain the three main checks on freedom of the press: prior restraint, libel law, and obscenity law.
6. Explain and distinguish between the establishment clause and the free exercise clause of the First Amendment.
7. Understand and explain the role of state militias in American history.
8. Explain how the Supreme Court has consistently interpreted the Second Amendment.
9. Explain what rights the Constitution gives to criminal suspects and to discuss how these rights limit what the government can do to fight crime.
10. Discuss the basis for the Supreme Court's decision that a right to privacy exists even though it is not specifically mentioned in the Constitution and show how the right to privacy formed the basis for the controversial *Roe v. Wade* decision declaring abortions in the first trimester to be constitutionally protected.

PRACTICE EXAM

(Answers appear at the end of this chapter)

Multiple Choice

1. Civil liberties are typically found in
    a. the Bill of Rights.
    b. acts of Congress.
    c. Supreme Court opinions.
    d. state legislation.

2. Who said that "The Constitution is what the judges say it is."
    a. Robert Bork
    b. Gregory Lee Johnson
    c. Charles Evan Hughes
    d. Sandra Day O'Connor

3. The meaning of the Constitution
    a. changes as justices come and go from the Supreme Court.
    b. changes as society changes.
    c. changes as presidents come and go.
    d. All of the above.

4. State governments
    a. are not bound by the Bill of Rights.
    b. have had to respect free speech since 1925.
    c. have always had to respect free speech.
    d. are not bound by the double jeopardy clause.

5. The Alien and Sedition Acts of 1798 made it illegal to
    a. publish obscene material.
    b. publish material that criticized the federal government.
    c. publish anything that interfered with defense production.
    d. publish material that promoted socialism.

6. The Supreme Court first utilized the clear and present danger standard in _____.
    a. *Schenck v. United States*
    b. *Near v. Minnesota*
    c. *New York Times Co. v. Sullivan*
    d. *Gideon v. Wainwright*

7. Town officials in Skokie, Illinois, violated the Nazis' right to
   a. privacy.
   b. free speech.
   c. religion.
   d. bear arms.

8. Prior restraint is used
   a. quite frequently.
   b. a great deal in the United States, but not very much in Iraq.
   c. only in exceptional cases.
   d. more by Democratic presidents than Republican presidents.

9. The establishment clause pertains to
   a. obscenity.
   b. speech.
   c. peaceful assembly.
   d. religion.

10. Prayer in the public schools
    a. is a policy supported by a strong majority of Americans.
    b. was banned by the Supreme Court in 1962.
    c. is a focal issue in the separation of church and state debate.
    d. All of the above.

11. How have the justices of the Supreme Court consistently interpreted the Second Amendment?
    a. Individuals have the right to bear arms.
    b. Individuals have a constitutional right to own a machine gun.
    c. It guarantees the people the right to maintain militias.
    d. Capital punishment is not cruel and unusual punishment.

12. Americans in the 1770s and 1780s
    a. deeply distrusted George Washington.
    b. deeply distrusted state militias.
    c. deeply distrusted a national army.
    d. None of the above.

13. What did the Supreme Court justices rule in *United States v. Cruikshank* (1876)?
    a. Slavery was unconstitutional.
    b. Gun ownership "is not a right guaranteed by the Constitution."
    c. Capital punishment does not violate the Eighth Amendment.
    d. Flag burning is protected under the Constitution.

14. The federal government
    a. places relatively few limits on gun ownership.
    b. has banned all assault weapons.
    c. failed to pass the Brady Bill.
    d. has adopted stringent gun-control laws compared to other industrialized nations.

15. The exclusionary rule
    a. gives the police an incentive to conduct proper searches.
    b. has never been applied to the states.
    c. forces the police to free many criminals on "technicalities."
    d. None of the above.

16. The Fifth Amendment
    a. protects individuals from self-incrimination.
    b. provides protection against double jeopardy.
    c. was the basis of the Supreme Court's adoption of the Miranda rights.
    d. All of the above.

17. As a result of *Gideon v. Wainwright* (1963),
    a. people accused of murder had the right to counsel, even if they could not afford an attorney.
    b. people accused of felonies had the right to counsel, even if they could not afford an attorney.
    c. the death penalty was abolished.
    d. the death penalty was reinstated.

18. The justices of the U.S. Supreme Court
    a. have never found the death penalty to be unconstitutional.
    b. ruled that the death penalty was imposed in an arbitrary, and therefore unconstitutional, manner in 1972.
    c. upheld a death penalty law in 1976 that had been rewritten in response to its objections in 1972.
    d. All of the above.

19. The right to privacy
    a. is implicit in the Bill of Rights.
    b. is cherished by the American people.
    c. is explicitly written in the Constitution.
    d. Both a and b.

20. The right to have a first trimester abortion is
    a. enumerated in the First Amendment.
    b. enumerated in the Fifth Amendment.
    c. implicitly protected in several places in the Constitution.
    d. universally accepted by American society.

Essays

21. How was the Bill of Rights broadened to include its application to state governments?
22. Why did the drafters of the Bill of Rights include the establishment and free exercise clauses in the First Amendment?
23. Does the Constitution give the people the right to bear arms? Explain.
24. Explain how the Supreme Court justices have interpreted the Eighth Amendment since the early 1970s.
25. How did the constitutional right to privacy evolve? Explain in contemporary terms, utilizing a concrete example.

CRITICAL THINKING EXERCISES

1. In a group of your peers, analyze the Supreme Court's most recent Constitutional interpretation of the following First Amendment issues:
    a.   Flag burning (*Texas v. Johnson*) 1989
    b.   Hate crimes (*R.A.V. v. St. Paul*) 1992
    What did the Supreme Court rule? Based on your interpretation of the Constitution, how would you have decided these cases? Why?

2. Trace the history of the Second Amendment. What was the intent of the amendment when it was added to the Constitution in 1791? Do you agree or disagree with Chief Justice Burger's criticism of the National Rifle Association (the Second Amendment "has been the subject of one of the greatest pieces of fraud, I repeat the word 'fraud,' on the American public"). Why or why not?

3. You are a justice on the Supreme Court. How would you interpret the Constitution? Would you follow a strict or broad interpretation, or something in-between? Would there be any ramifications for society? Explain.

ANSWERS TO THE PRACTICE EXAM

1.	A	11.	C
2.	C	12.	C
3.	D	13.	B
4.	B	14.	A
5.	B	15.	A
6.	A	16.	D
7.	B	17.	B
8.	C	18.	D
9.	D	19.	D
10.	D	20.	C

21. When the Bill of Rights was adopted, it only applied to the relations between the people and the federal government. Gradually, around the turn of the century, the justices of the Supreme Court began applying the Bill of Rights to the states. This was prompted by the passage of the Fourteenth Amendment in 1868, which declares that no state shall "deprive any person of life, liberty, or property, without due process of law."

The Supreme Court ruled that states had to guarantee free speech in 1925, and many other provisions in the Bill of Rights have been applied to the states since then.

22. The establishment and free exercise clauses were intended to keep the government separate from religion and to allow Americans to practice the religion of their choice. They are both reflective of political realities, as well as theories about individual rights. Even at that time, Americans worshiped many different denominations, thus making it imperative to forbid the federal government from creating an official state church, such as the Church of England in Britain, and from banning some religions while allowing the exercise of others to be sanctioned.

23. Although the vast majority of Americans believes that the Constitution gives them the right to own guns, the Supreme Court has never recognized such a constitutional right. The Second Amendment states that "A well regulated Militia, being necessary to the security of a free state, the right of the people to keep and bear Arms, shall not be infringed." Instead of granting individuals the right to keep and bear arms, the Court has long held that the Second Amendment only guarantees to states the right to maintain militias without excessive interference by the federal government. Thus despite contentions by the National Rifle Association, the Court has never recognized the private ownership of guns as an inalienable right guaranteed by the Second Amendment.

24. The Supreme Court justices have never found capital punishment, the death penalty, to be cruel and unusual under the Eighth Amendment. In 1972, the Court did rule that death sentences were being imposed in an arbitrary, and therefore unconstitutional, manner. In 1976, however, the justices upheld a death penalty law that had been rewritten in response to its objections in 1972. Since the late 1970s, the number of executions has increased, and the public has maintained its support in favor of capital punishment. Recent cases have dealt with how the death penalty is implemented. The justices have ruled that someone as young as sixteen years old may be put to death, the Court has also ruled that a mentally retarded person could be executed but not a person who is legally insane.

25. Although the Constitution does not mention privacy, there are hints of it in the Bill of Rights. In *Griswold v. Connecticut* (1965), the Supreme Court invalidated a Connecticut law forbidding the use of birth control. The justices found a right to privacy in several places in the Constitution: the First Amendment's right to association, the Third Amendment's prohibition against the quartering of soldiers, the Fourth Amendment's ban on unreasonable searches and seizures, the Fifth Amendment's protection against self-incrimination, and the Ninth Amendment's provision that the Constitution did not enumerate all individual rights. In *Griswold*, the justices ruled that the zone of privacy allows married couples the right to use contraceptives. This was later extended to include unmarried persons as well. The right to privacy was extended to include first trimester abortions in *Roe v. Wade* (1973).

Chapter 5 Civil Rights

SUMMARY

Civil rights are legal and moral claims that citizens are entitled to make on their government. Even after the Fourteenth Amendment was ratified in 1868, many minorities were denied equal protection of the law. The civil rights movement involved forcing Congress and the Supreme Court to fully implement this fundamental liberty. Yet the very success of the movement at ensuring equality has created new tensions. The most obvious conflict centers around affirmative action programs, and will undoubtedly be addressed by new rules promulgated by the Supreme Court.

OUTLINE

Opening Story: Affirmative Action and the University of California Board of Regents

The University of California Regents met in the summer of 1995 to consider a proposal to end thirty years of racial and gender-based preferences in admissions, hiring, and contracting. Over three decades, these preferences resulted in a substantial increase in the number of women and minorities attending and working at the nine campuses in the California system. Yet in the nation's most ethnically diverse state, these preferences were under harsh criticism, and a petition drive was under way to put a proposition on the state ballot to end all racial and gender-based preferences at the state and local level. Public opinion polls demonstrated that the measure had broad support. Governor Pete Wilson, a member of the Board of Regents, was making his opposition to preferences a major plank in his bid to capture the Republican nomination for U.S. president. After a tumultuous debate, the regents voted in favor of ending racial and gender-based preferences in admissions, hiring, and contracting.

Civil Liberties and Civil Rights (p. 127)

Discrimination against African Americans (p. 128)

From Slavery to Emancipation (p. 128)

Jim Crow (p. 130)

The First Civil Rights Organizations (p. 133)

The Brown Decision (p. 135)

The Civil Rights Movement (p. 138)

Congress Responds (p. 139)

The Continuing Fight against Discrimination (p. 141)

Discrimination against Asian Americans, Hispanic Americans, American Indians, and Others (p. 143)

Asian Americans (p. 143)

Hispanic Americans (p. 146)

American Indians (p. 146)

Other Minorities (p. 148)

Discrimination against Women (p. 148)

Campaigning for the Right to Vote (p. 149)

The Fight for Equal Rights on Capitol Hill (p. 150)

The Fight for Equal Rights in the Courts (p. 153)

The Continuing Struggle against Sex Discrimination (p. 154)

Extending Civil Rights (p. 156)

People with Disabilities (p. 156)

People with Age Claims (p. 157)

Gays and Lesbians (p. 157)

The Burden of Proof (p. 160)

Affirmative Action: Equal Opportunity or Equal Outcomes? (p. 160)

Summary (p. 164)

Key Terms (p. 165)

Readings for Further Study (p. 165)

KEY TERMS, CONCEPTS, EVENTS, AND PEOPLE

Be able to identify and/or define each of the following and state its importance in a short paragraph.

Civil rights (p. 127)

Jim Crow laws (p. 131)

De jure segregation (p. 131)

"Separate-but-equal" standard (p. 131)

Lynching (p. 133)

Brown v. Board of Education (p. 135)

Brown v. Board of Education II (p. 136)

Massive resistance (p. 136)

Civil rights movement (p. 138)

Civil disobedience (p. 138)

Civil Rights Act of 1964 (p. 140)

Voting Rights Act of 1965 (p. 140)

De facto segregation (p. 141)

Women's movement (p. 149)

Suffrage (p. 149)

Equal Pay Act of 1963 (p. 151)

Americans with Disabilities Act of 1990 (p. 156)

Rational scrutiny (p. 160)

Strict scrutiny (p. 160)

Intermediate scrutiny (p. 160)

Affirmative action (p. 160)

Reverse discrimination (p. 162)

LEARNING OBJECTIVES

After reading chapter 5, students should be able to:

1. Explain the difference between civil liberties and civil rights.
2. Describe the history of the African-American struggle for civil rights.
3. Explain the adoption of the post-Civil War constitutional amendments and the rise of Jim Crow laws.
4. Discuss the landmark Supreme Court decisions of *Plessy v. Ferguson* and *Brown v. Board of Education*.
5. Discuss the importance of the Civil Rights Act of 1964 and the Voting Rights Act of 1965.
6. Describe the history of discrimination in the United States against Asian Americans and discuss some of the major Supreme Court rulings affecting Asian Americans.
7. Describe the history of discrimination in the United States against Hispanic Americans and discuss some of the major Supreme Court rulings affecting Asian Americans.
8. Describe the history of discrimination in the United States against American Indians and discuss some of the major Supreme Court rulings affecting Asian Americans.
9. Describe the history of the women's rights movement in the United States, including the adoption of the Nineteenth Amendment in 1920, the passage of the Equal Pay Act of 1963, and the failure of the proposed Equal Rights Amendment to the Constitution.
10. Discuss how Congress sought to guarantee and protect the civil rights of people with physical and mental disabilities by passing the Americans with Disabilities Act of 1990.
11. Explain the problems of discrimination on the basis of age against both the young and the elderly and discuss some of the actions Congress has taken to protect against age discrimination.
12. Discuss the efforts by gays and lesbians to win legal recognition of their civil rights.
13. Define what affirmative action is and to describe the debate over how far affirmative action programs should go to ensure equality.

PRACTICE EXAM

(Answers appear at the end of this chapter)

Multiple Choice

1. Congress made the importation of slaves illegal in
   _____.
   a. 1787
   b. 1808
   c. 1828
   d. 1857

2. The Thirteenth Amendment _____, and was ratified in _____.
   a. banned alcohol, 1919
   b. allowed for direct election of U.S. senators, 1913
   c. banned slavery, 1865
   d. gave women the right to vote, 1920

3. What was Reconstruction?
   a. The period of time when federal troops occupied the South (1865-1877).
   b. The period of time when Abraham Lincoln was president (1861-1865).
   c. The period of time when Rutherford B. Hayes was president (1877-1881).
   d. None of the above.

4. The "separate-but-equal" standard was promulgated by the Supreme Court justices in
   a. *Dred Scott v. Sandford* (1857).
   b. *Plessy v. Ferguson* (1896).
   c. *Brown v. Board of Education* (1954).
   d. *Brown v. Board of Education II* (1955).

5. Who said "segregation now, segregation tomorrow, segregation forever"?
   a. James Meredith
   b. John F. Kennedy
   c. Martin Luther King, Jr.
   d. George Wallace

6. _____ started the civil rights movement in 1955 in Montgomery, Alabama.
   a. Rosa Parks
   b. Martin Luther King, Jr.
   c. Jesse Jackson
   d. James Meredith

7. Segregation denies minorities
   a. their rights under the First Amendment.
   b. their rights under the Fourteenth Amendment's equal protection clause.
   c. their rights under the Civil Rights Act of 1957.
   d. their rights under the Jim Crow laws.

8. _____ outlawed segregation in public accommodations, barred tax dollars from going to organizations that discriminated on the basis of race, color, or national origin, and created the Equal Employment Opportunity Commission.
   a. The Civil Rights Act of 1957
   b. The Voting Rights Act of 1965
   c. The Civil Rights Act of 1964
   d. The Civil Rights Act of 1991

9. Who organized the "Million Man March" in October, 1995, which is considered the largest civil rights demonstration in U.S. history?
   a. Jesse Jackson
   b. Colin Powell
   c. Louis Farrakhan
   d. Clarence Thomas

10. During World War II, _____ Americans living on the West Coast were relocated and forced to live in detention camps.
    a. German
    b. Italian
    c. Japanese
    d. German, Italian, and Japanese

11. _____ were not granted citizenship by Congress until 1924.
    a. African Americans
    b. Asian Americans
    c. Hispanic Americans
    d. Native Americans

12. _____ organized the first women's rights convention in Seneca Falls, New York in 1848.
    a. Susan B. Anthony
    b. Jeanette Rankin
    c. Elizabeth Cady Stanton and Lucretia Mott
    d. Margaret Chase Smith

13. Women were granted the right to vote nationally in
    a. 1870.
    b. 1920.
    c. 1945.
    d. 1971.

14. _____ wrote *The Feminine Mystique*, which partly inspired the reemergence of the women's movement in the 1960s?
    a. Betty Friedan
    b. Gloria Steinem
    c. Howard Smith
    d. Molly Yard

15. _____ was the first president to openly endorse gay rights legislation.
    a. Jimmy Carter
    b. Ronald Reagan
    c. George Bush
    d. Bill Clinton

16. Under _____, the burden of proof rests with the individual or group challenging the government to prove that a law is unreasonable or arbitrary.
   a. rational scrutiny
   b. intermediate scrutiny
   c. strict scrutiny
   d. liberal scrutiny

17. The affirmative action movement began under President
   a. John Kennedy.
   b. Lyndon Johnson.
   c. Richard Nixon.
   d. Jimmy Carter.

18. The Supreme Court justices
   a. upheld the use of quotas as constitutional in the *Bakke* decision.
   b. ruled that the use of quotas was unconstitutional in the *Bakke* decision.
   c. have never ruled on the constitutionality of quotas.
   d. have always ruled that racial set-aside programs are constitutional.

19. Affirmative action programs
   a. are designed to increase the number of women and minorities in jobs and education.
   b. always guarantee equal outcomes.
   c. began in the 1930s in the New Deal.
   d. were ended by the Clinton Administration.

20. _____ have largely been unable to gain specific coverage under U.S. civil rights laws.
   a. African Americans
   b. Americans with disabilities
   c. Asian Americans
   d. Gay and lesbian Americans

Essays

21. What were some of the political tactics and strategies utilized by advocates of civil rights in the 1950s and 1960s? Explain.
22. When was the Fifteenth Amendment, which gave African-American males the right to vote in 1870, fully implemented by the U.S. government? Explain.
23. Explain how the Supreme Court's interpretation of the Fourteenth Amendment's equal protection clause changed from 1896 to 1954.
24. Detail the plight of equal rights amendment proposals, both at the federal and state levels.
25. Why does equality of opportunity often conflict with equality of outcome? Explain in contemporary terms, utilizing a concrete example.

CRITICAL THINKING EXERCISES

1. In a group of your peers, discuss and debate the following question: In the United States today, are all citizens treated equally in society? Why or why not? Be able to provide concrete illustrations to support your perspective.
2. Does slavery exist anywhere in the world today? If so, where and how did you find out about it?
3. What are your views on affirmative action programs? Should these programs be maintained, abolished, or reformed in some way? Is this a just policy, or not? Explain.

ANSWERS TO THE PRACTICE EXAM

1.	B	11.	D
2.	C	12.	C
3.	A	13.	B
4.	B	14.	A
5.	D	15.	D
6.	A	16.	A
7.	B	17.	B
8.	C	18.	B
9.	C	19.	A
10.	C	20.	D

21. The civil rights movement began in 1955 by a single act of defiance. Rosa Parks, a member of the NAACP in Montgomery, Alabama, boarded a city bus in a seat in front that was reserved for whites. In so doing, she was violating a city ordinance and was arrested and fined. This led to the Montgomery boycott, where African Americans boycotted the city's busses for more than a year, and which ultimately led to an affirmation by the Supreme Court that laws requiring segregation on city busses were unconstitutional. The Montgomery boycott thrust Martin Luther King, Jr., the leader of the Southern Christian Leadership Conference, into the national spotlight. He advocated the idea of civil disobedience, the nonviolent refusal to obey unjust laws, as a means to force an end to racial discrimination. One type of civil disobedience was the sit-in (beginning with the Greensboro sit-in, in 1960). Another tactic born in the summer of 1961 were the "freedom rides." They were intended to pressure government to desegregate public facilities such as bus stations. The protest march was also employed to promote the cause of African-American rights. In addition to practicing civil disobedience, leaders in the civil rights movement also worked within the law to promote the rights of African Americans. Paramount in this effort was the effort to register African Americans to vote, a successful endeavor that was unfortunately met with a great deal of resistance and violence by whites, particularly in the South.

22. Although the Fifteenth Amendment was added to the U.S. Constitution in 1870, its promise was not fully implemented by the U.S. government until Congress passed the Voting Rights Act of 1965. The Voting Rights Act outlawed most registration and voting practices which discriminated against African Americans and other minorities. Perhaps most importantly, it gave the Justice Department authority to review registration and voting laws in states in which less than 50% of the population was registered. Since 1965, there has been a dramatic increase in the number of African Americans registered to vote. The number of African Americans elected to political office has also increased, especially at the local level.

23. In 1896, the Supreme Court's majority adopted the "separate but equal" standard in *Plessy v. Ferguson*. Many state laws segregated public facilities by race. In this case, the Court upheld segregated public facilities, and ruled that segregated public facilities were acceptable and did not violate the Fourteenth Amendment's equal protection clause as long as they were "equal." Most prominent among the public facilities where segregation was sanctioned were public school systems. By 1954, the justices completely reversed the *Plessy* decision. In *Brown v. Board of Education*, the justices ruled that separate but equal was "inherently unequal." School segregation, according to the Court, violated the equal protection clause of the Fourteenth Amendment. Thus, 58 years after the fact, the American system of apartheid was formally rejected by the government.

24. By 1972, both houses of Congress passed the Equal Rights Amendment, which simply stated: "Equality of rights under the law shall not be denied or abridged by the United States or by any state on account of sex." Within a couple of years, thirty-five state legislatures ratified the ERA (under the Constitution, three-fourths of the state legislatures must ratify an amendment proposal, or thirty-eight of the fifty states). The ERA failed to become a part of the Constitution as it failed to garner the approval of the three additional states needed for ratification. At the state level, sixteen states have an equal rights provision in their state constitution.

In recent years, however, supporters of the ERA have failed to make additional progress. Voters in Iowa, for example, rejected a proposal to add an equal rights amendment to their state constitution in 1992.

25.   The issue that most clearly illustrates the conflict between equality of opportunity and equality of outcome is affirmative action. The affirmative action movement began in the mid 1960s as an attempt to increase the number of women and minorities in jobs and education. Historically, women and minorities have been discriminated against in both sectors. As a result, both women and racial minorities are underrepresented in the workplace and in education. Most Americans support the concept of equal opportunity—all persons should have the same chance to obtain employment. Furthermore, most people agree that white males, in particular, have had distinct advantages in these areas. The conflict arises when the debate centers on the rules—do we need to make rules that try to ensure equal opportunity? Do we need to establish rules that guarantee equal outcomes? Proponents of affirmative action argue that only positive actions can redress the negative effects of decades of discrimination. Opponents contend that affirmative action creates a system of reverse discrimination, in which whites (especially males) are denied equal protection under the law. The government has the cumbersome task of creating rules that somehow balance the two sets of rights. This has proven to be a difficult task indeed.

SUMMARY

In a democracy, the people rule. Elected representatives are supposed to make policy based on the will of the people. Yet the nature of public opinion makes public policy-making a very complex process. Large majorities of Americans know very little about their own government. Most Americans do not have detailed information about a variety of policy issues, although the vast majority has at least some knowledge about selected political issues.

Translating public opinion into public policy is even more difficult for officials because knowledge is not distributed equally in American society. Those who are better educated and have higher incomes know a good deal more about politics than the rest of the population.

Mixed messages are often sent to elected representatives from the public. Since public opinion can be very difficult to decipher precisely, it should only be thought of as an approximate guide to public policy. It is simply too vague in many cases, and as a result, political parties and vested interest groups often act as intermediaries between the people and their government.

OUTLINE

Opening Story: The Contract with America and Public Opinion

Prior to the 1994 congressional elections, America's newspapers were filled with stories about the "Contract with America," a ten-point platform supported by Republican candidates for the House of Representatives. House Republican leaders had the Contract published in *TV Guide*, the magazine with the largest readership in the U.S. In spite of the enormous media coverage, both on television and in the print media, most Americans had very little or no substantive knowledge of the Republican's Contract. In fact, one public opinion poll conducted after the November election determined that 72% of the public had never heard of the Contract with America. As this example demonstrates, the public lacks knowledge about many issues that government officials must confront.

The People's Limited Knowledge of Politics (p. 170)

The Distribution of Knowledge (p. 174)

Sources of Knowledge (p. 176)

People with Knowledge: Issue Publics (p. 176)

The Nature and Acquisition of Opinions and Values (p. 177)

Family and Friends (p. 177)

School (p. 178)

The Media (p. 179)

Lifetime Learning (p. 180)

Ideologies (p. 180)

Liberalism (p. 181)

Conservatism (p. 183)

Changes Over Time (p. 183)

Sources of Ideologies (p. 185)

The Process of Molding Ideologies (p. 186)

Public Opinion on the Issues (p. 187)

Ideological Thinking by the Public (p. 187)

Abstract Symbols Versus Concrete Policies (p. 188)

Public Opinion on Clusters of Related Issues (p. 190)

Changes in Opinion Over Time (p. 195)

Causes of Change (p. 196)

Summary (p. 197)

Key Terms (p. 198)

Readings for Further Study (p. 198)

KEY TERMS, CONCEPTS, EVENTS, AND PEOPLE

Be able to identify and/or define each of the following and state its importance in a short paragraph.

Public opinion (p. 170)

Socioeconomic status (p. 175)

Political efficacy (p. 175)

42

Attentive publics or issue publics (p. 176)

Opinions or attitudes (p. 177)

Values (p. 177)

Socialization (p. 177)

Ideology (p. 180)

Liberalism (p. 181)

Conservatism (p. 181)

Capitalism (p. 181)

Left (p. 181)

Right (p. 183)

Prohibition (p. 186)

Women's or feminist movement (p. 186)

Attitude consistency (p. 187)

Economic issues (p. 190)

Social issues (p. 190)

Pro-choice (p. 193)

Pro-life (p. 193)

LEARNING OBJECTIVES

After reading chapter 6, students should be able to:

1. Recognize that the public generally does not know much about politics.
2. Discuss the demographic and social roots of political knowledge.
3. Recognize that newspaper reading is declining, while television news viewing is increasing, and that newspapers are far more informative than television news.
4. Define what issue publics are and discuss why politicians pay more attention to issue publics than to other less informed citizens.
5. Discuss how people acquire opinions from family, friends, schools, and the media through socialization.
6. Define and distinguish between the ideologies of liberalism and conservatism.
7. Discuss how ideologies change over time in response to changing group interests.
8. Defend and distinguish between the ideologies of liberalism and conservatism.
9. Discuss how most Americans display a fairly low level of ideological thinking, as measured by attitude consistency.
10. Explain how different measures of the public's ideological views often yield different assessments of how liberal or conservative the public is—especially when the public's support for abstract statements is compared with the public's support for concrete government programs.
11. Distinguish between economic and social issues.
12. Explain how the demographic patterns of support for liberal and conservative positions on economic and social issues varies.
13. Discuss how opinions on specific issues are generally stable over time.
14. Discuss how opinions on social issues have become more liberal since World War II and show that opinions on economic issues have had mixed trends.
15. Explain how most trends in public opinion can be traced to social or economic forces, but that individuals and organizations play important leadership roles.

PRACTICE EXAM

(Answers appear at the end of this chapter)

Multiple Choice

1. How might one explain the public's limited knowledge about politics?
    a. People are basically stupid.
    b. The media does not provide enough information to the people.
    c. The government does not provide enough information to the media, which reports it to the people.
    d. For most people, politics is not important.

2. In a 1995 survey by *The Washington Post*, _____% of Americans indicated that the fictitious "1975 Public Affairs Act" should be repealed?
    a. 0
    b. 12
    c. 43
    d. 86

3. In order to gauge the public opinion of adults in America within plus or minus 3.1%, how many people need to be surveyed to render an accurate assessment?
    a. 250
    b. 1,000
    c. 5,000
    d. 10,000

4. Knowledge about politics
    a. is spread uniformly across the public.
    b. is greater for working class people.
    c. is strongly associated with education.
    d. is greater for the working poor.

5. The primary source of news for most Americans is
   a. the daily newspaper.
   b. television.
   c. the news weekly.
   d. the tabloid newspaper.

6. Issue publics
   a. do not have much influence on the political process.
   b. typically include people without a high school diploma.
   c. typically include people with high incomes and good jobs.
   d. tend not to influence governmental policy very much.

7. How do people acquire their values and opinions?
   a. Media
   b. Family and friends
   c. School
   d. All of the above

8. Which two political ideologies are most widespread in America today?
   a. Liberalism and Conservatism
   b. Marxism and Socialism
   c. Republicanism and Democratism
   d. Libertarianism and Anarchism

9. Liberals believe that government should take an active role in moving society toward
   a. equality of opportunities.
   b. equality of outcomes.
   c. Socialism.
   d. Marxism.

10. Jesse Helms and Pat Buchanan are examples of contemporary
    a. liberals.
    b. moderates.
    c. conservatives.
    d. None of the above.

11. During the Prohibition era, Yankee Protestants and ethnic European Catholics battled over
    a. rules.
    b. campaign finance reform.
    c. religious differences.
    d. the fundamental right to privacy.

12. Describe attitude consistency in the United States.
    a. People tend to think in ideological terms.
    b. People tend to have a weak understanding of different philosophies.
    c. People tend to have a good understanding of different philosophies.
    d. People tend to either be liberal or conservative, but not moderate.

13. Which of the following groups is *most likely* to support tax cuts and flatter tax rates?
    a. People with an income between 0-$19,999.
    b. People who have not graduated from high school.
    c. People with an income greater than $50,000.
    d. People who support the Democratic Party.

14. Which of the following groups is *most likely* to support homosexual rights?
    a. People who are older than 50.
    b. People who have an income between 0-$19,999.
    c. People who have graduated from college.
    d. People who have not graduated from high school.

15. Conservatives believe that the government should play a minimal role in society, except on the issue of
    a. raising the minimum wage.
    b. increasing social welfare benefits.
    c. regulating the operation of businesses.
    d. abortion.

16. Attitudes on economic issues are heavily influenced by
    a. education.
    b. ideology.
    c. economic self-interest.
    d. the editorial section of newspapers.

17. Attitudes on social issues are heavily influenced by
    a. economic self-interest.
    b. education.
    c. the editorial section of newspapers.
    d. political party preference.

18. For the most part, public opinion
    a. is almost always destined to become more conservative.
    b. is fairly stable over time.
    c. is fairly unstable over time.
    d. is almost always destined to become more liberal.

19. Most movements in public opinion can be attributed to
    a. social forces.
    b. economic forces.
    c. the leadership of important officials.
    d. All of the above.

20. The history of public opinion in America over the last 50 years demonstrates that
    a. the public has become more conservative on social issues, and more liberal on economic issues.
    b. the public has become more liberal on social issues, and more conservative on economic issues.
    c. the public has become more liberal on social issues, and that trends on economic issues have been mixed.
    d. the public has become more liberal on both social and economic issues.

Essays

21. Is knowledge about politics uniformly distributed across the public? Explain why or why not. Is this important? Explain.
22. What impact does the mass media have on the socialization process?
23. How do the central principles of liberalism and conservatism differ? Apply what you know about the two ideologies to the issue of abortion. Do liberals and conservatives contradict their own philosophies on this issue? Explain.
24. Explain the contradictory nature of the ideological thinking of the American public.
25. How should elected government officials contend with the issue of public opinion in making public policies?

CRITICAL THINKING EXERCISES

1. Test your own knowledge about current political leaders: give yourself 10 points for each correct response (your instructor and/or reference librarian at your school can assist you in finding the correct information). Identify the individuals who currently hold the following positions:
    a. Speaker of the U.S. House of Representatives
    b. Majority Leader of the U.S. Senate
    c. Minority Leader of the U.S. Senate
    d. Governor of your state
    e. Two U.S. Senators from your state
    f. Your congressional representative (U.S. House of Representatives)
    g. Secretary of State
    h. Secretary of Treasury
    i. Secretary of Defense
    j. U.S. Attorney General

2. Write an essay entitled "My political socialization." Include a discussion of all relevant factors that have contributed to the manner in which you have developed your values and opinions about politics.

3. In a typical week, count how many hours a week you watch television. Compare that to how many hours a week you spend in the classroom AND studying. What is the ratio? Compare your ratio with that of some of your peers. Also, take note of what you watch and compare this to the programs viewed by your peers. After doing this, assess your viewing habits. Are you satisfied with your management of time, or are there any habitual changes that you need to undertake to manage your time more effectively? Simply do a little self-reflection on these issues.

ANSWERS TO THE PRACTICE EXAM

1.	D	11.	A
2.	C	12.	B
3.	B	13.	C
4.	C	14.	C
5.	B	15.	D
6.	C	16.	C
7.	D	17.	B
8.	A	18.	B
9.	B	19.	D
10.	C	20.	C

21.   Knowledge about politics is not uniformly distributed across the public. Some groups are far more knowledgeable than others. People are more likely to learn about politics if they have the opportunity to learn, the capacity to learn, and an interest in learning about the subject. There are demographic, social, and psychological characteristics that are related to political knowledge. The most important demographic traits are high levels of education, income, and occupational status. Social characteristics such as being active in an organization help make individuals more cognizant of politics as well. Finally, psychological characteristics, especially interest in politics and a sense of political efficacy, lead to greater levels of knowledge as well. The uneven distribution of knowledge is very important, because knowledge itself is a political resource. Individuals and groups that possess political knowledge are able to wield political power, those that do not tend not to have much influence on the political process.

22.   The mass media is another source of socialization. Its impact on the socialization process can be powerful, as many children begin watching television when they are infants. The average American student spends more time watching television than in the classroom. Heavy consumers of the mass media tend to hold the moderate political views typically portrayed on television. The mass media can influence the socialization process in many ways. Women, racial, and ethnic minorities have been stereotyped in television programming and in the movies. As a result, people acquire mistaken impressions of facts from the entertainment industry. Furthermore, violence is depicted at far greater levels on television and in the movies than what truly exists in society. As a result, many people exaggerate the crime problem, and demand more police, more prisons, and longer prison sentences for criminals from their elected officials. Entertainment affects the public's perceptions of society. In turn, public policy is indirectly affected through public opinion.

23.   The central principle of contemporary liberalism is that the government ought to play an extensive role in society with the goal of protecting its poorer and weaker citizens. Liberals believe that government should take an active role in moving society toward equality of outcomes. The central principle of conservatism, on the other hand, is that government ought to play a minimal role in society, except to uphold traditional moral standards. In economic matters, conservatives believe that government should be limited to ensuring equality of opportunities, and not outcomes. On the issue of abortion, practicing liberals and conservatives do seem to contradict their respective central principles. Many liberals believe that the government should stay out of privacy issues, and therefore contend that abortion is protected in the Constitution under the right to privacy. On the abortion issue, liberals are often called pro-choice. Many conservatives believe that government should play an expansive role in social matters, believing that majorities ought to be able to limit personal behavior on moral grounds. As a result, many conservatives have adopted the pro-life stance.

24.   In public opinion polls, Americans have demonstrated a consistent pattern of both supporting conservative symbols and liberal policies at the same time. Americans are opposed to "big government," yet they are supportive of government spending in a wide variety of social policy issues. This mix of liberal and conservative opinions stems from the public's relative apathy and lack of substantive political knowledge. Few understand the connections between abstract statements such as "free enterprise" and support for government

programs. One belief implies less government intervention in the marketplace, while the other implies more government intervention. As a result, most people cannot be described as either very liberal or very conservative. The majority of Americans can be described as moderate, while most people in fact have a mix of liberal, moderate, and conservative opinions.

25. For elected government officials, taking public opinion into account when making public policies can be very difficult. Most people are lacking in substantive political knowledge. On many issues, the public sends mixed messages. While we live in a democracy where the people rule through their elected representatives, public opinion should only be considered as an approximate guide to government policy. Public opinion is often difficult to decipher in the precise terms required for making public policy, so as a result officials should consider public opinion just one of numerous factors when creating and implementing policies governing the country.

SUMMARY

The rules governing elections allow all Americans the opportunity to vote and participate in the political process. Rules, however, do not guarantee that all persons will choose to engage in these activities. As a result, it is oftentimes difficult to ascertain whether the will of the people is reflected in the candidate who actually wins. This is particularly true in the United States, where only slightly higher than half of the electorate will exercise its right to vote in a presidential election. Turnout is even lower in non-presidential election years.

There are many factors involved in winning an election: who votes (typically people with high incomes, good educations, and high-status jobs); the laws governing voter registration in each state; the effectiveness of the campaign; people's preferences about party labels, candidate characteristics, and the issues; the strategies taken by the candidates; and the coverage by the mass media. In the American electoral system, the people, politicians, journalists, and the rules under which they compete all play important roles in who wins and who loses in any given election.

OUTLINE

Opening Story: Voting and Participation in the 1996 Presidential Election

Even with the extensive coverage of the campaign from its beginning in the Iowa Caucuses and the New Hampshire primary through the November election, the fact that millions of dollars were spent, and a veritable army of campaign workers crossed the entire country, only slightly better than half of all eligible voters bothered to cast a ballot in the pivotal 1996 presidential election. Even though the outcome of the election could have fundamentally changed the direction of our nation's public policy in a more conservative manner, the American people did not seem to truly recognize its importance. In the midst of a national debate about the future of the American democracy, politics remained of little interest to many citizens.

In a democracy, the central activity is voting, yet most people do not participate in elections. Who chooses to participate and who chooses not to greatly influences which candidates win and what policies become law. The demographics and characteristics of individual people, as well as the rules of the political system, determine who participates.

Who Votes (p. 202)

The Effects of Individual Voter Characteristics (p. 202)

The Effect of Registration Laws (p. 206)

The Effect of Campaign Contacts (p. 208)

The Puzzling Decline of Voter Turnout (p. 212)

Does Turnout Matter? (p. 214)

Political Activists (p. 215)

Who Becomes an Activist? (p. 215)

Types of Activists (p. 216)

How Voters Make Choices (p. 217)

Party Identification (p. 217)

Candidate Characteristics (p. 220)

Issues (p. 221)

Changes Over Time (p. 225)

Voting and Social Groups (p. 226)

Summary (p. 228)

Key Terms (p. 229)

Readings for Further Study (p. 230)

KEY TERMS, CONCEPTS, EVENTS, AND PEOPLE

Be able to identify and/or define each of the following and state its importance in a short paragraph.

Voter turnout (p. 202)

Franchise (p. 204)

Group consciousness (p. 205)

Closing date (p. 207)

Poll tax (p. 208)

Literacy test (p. 208)

Australian ballot (p. 213)

Party identification (p. 217)

Candidate characteristics (p. 220)

Retrospective issue voting (p. 221)

Prospective issue voting (p. 222)

Sociotropic voters (p. 222)

Easy issues (p. 224)

Hard issues (p. 224)

Gender gap (p. 227)

LEARNING OBJECTIVES

After reading chapter 7, students should be able to:

1. Discuss the demographic and social factors that influence voter turnout.
2. Explain the effects of voter registration and other legal/institutional factors on voter turnout.
3. Evaluate the conflicting explanations for the declines in voter turnout following the elections of 1896 and 1960.
4. Recognize that the overall level of political activism is very low and discuss the types and causes of activism.
5. Explain the concept of party identification and discuss its measurement and effects.
6. Explain how citizens' evaluations of candidate characteristics influence their voting choices and discuss how some voter prejudices remain.
7. Define what constitutes retrospective issue voting and assess how it affects elections.
8. Define what constitutes prospective issue voting and identify the four necessary conditions for issue voting.
9. Distinguish between "hard" and "easy" issues and discuss their roles in issue voting.
10. Explain how the influence of party identification, candidate characteristics, and issues can change from one election to the next.
11. Identify the voting patterns of different social groups.

PRACTICE EXAM

(Answers appear at the end of this chapter)

Multiple Choice

1. Voter turnout depends on
   a. individual voter characteristics.
   b. registration laws.
   c. campaign contacts.
   d. All of the above.

2. What is the MOST important variable which explains whether or not a person votes?
   a. Political efficacy
   b. Race and ethnicity
   c. Age
   d. Education

3. Compared to most other democracies in the world,
   a. the United States has a high level of voter turnout.
   b. the United States is about in the middle in terms of voter turnout.
   c. the United States has a low level of voter turnout.
   d. the United States typically has a voter turnout rate exceeding 70 percent.

4. States with Election Day registration have _____ turnout than states that close off registration thirty days before the election.
   a. higher
   b. lower
   c. basically the same
   d. None of the above

5. The Twenty-fourth Amendment abolished
   _____.
   a. slavery
   b. poll taxes
   c. literacy tests
   d. grandfather clauses

6. The 1965 Voting Rights Act
   a. helped to increase registration and voter turnout by minorities.
   b. helped to force the Klu Klux Klan to dissolve.
   c. helped to increase discrimination against minorities in the South.
   d. helped precinct workers assist voters on Election Day.

7. Most people participate in politics by
   a. donating money to a political candidate.
   b. attending political rallies.
   c. working for a political campaign.
   d. voting.

8. Which of the following is MOST likely to be a political activist?
   a. 55 year old corporate lawyer
   b. 25 year old unemployed factory worker
   c. 19 year old student
   d. 46 year old janitor

9. According to a 1994 poll, which political party is favored by more Americans?
   a. Republican
   b. Independent
   c. Democratic
   d. Socialist

10. Which of the following is an "easy" issue?
    a. Health care
    b. Budget deficit
    c. Abortion
    d. Immigration

11. Party identification
    a. influences issue preferences.
    b. caused some people to believe Bill Clinton, and others to believe Paula Jones.
    c. helps people to interpret politics.
    d. All of the above.

12. What is the conventional wisdom regarding retrospective voting?
    a. Most people vote their pocketbooks.
    b. Most people are influenced by their community's needs.
    c. Most people vote for a cleaner environment.
    d. Most people vote to reduce the number of nuclear weapons.

13. In the 1992 presidential election,
    a. retrospective voting played a large role in George Bush's defeat.
    b. George Bush suffered because many people thought that the economy was doing poorly.
    c. Bill Clinton received a lot of support from people who believed that the economy was doing poorly.
    d. All of the above.

14. When it comes to issue voting,
    a. most Americans have a good understanding of the issues.
    b. hard issues tend to dominate election debates.
    c. prospective issue voting is a dominant factor in voting decisions.
    d. most Americans tend to look to the past, and not to the future.

15. In the 1992 presidential election, which of the following groups was most supportive of Bill Clinton?
    a. White Protestants
    b. Those making $75,000 or more
    c. African Americans
    d. College graduates

16. In the 1992 presidential election, which of the following groups was most supportive of George Bush?
    a. Catholics
    b. Those making $15,000-$29,999
    c. Conservatives
    d. Those with a high school diploma

17. In the 1992 presidential election, which of the following groups was most supportive of Ross Perot?
    a. Whites
    b. African Americans
    c. Women
    d. Jews

18. Since the late 1970s, women have been slightly more likely
    a. to support Republican candidates than men.
    b. to support Democratic candidates than men.
    c. to support increasing the size of the military.
    d. to support cuts in social welfare programs.

19. Winning elections is contingent upon
    a. who votes.
    b. campaign strategies.
    c. the issues.
    d. All of the above.

20. Which of the following influences voting decisions the MOST?
    a. Issues
    b. Candidate characteristics
    c. Party identification
    d. Political climate

Essays

21. What factors help analysts explain who votes and who does not in American elections?
22. How can state registration laws affect voter turnout? Explain.
23. Describe the puzzling decline of voter turnout since 1896. What are some of the theories offered by scholars to help explain this phenomenon?
24. When Americans choose and then vote for a candidate, what factors largely influence their choices? Explain.
25. Which social groups tend to favor the Democratic Party, and which groups tend to be more supportive of the Republican Party?

CRITICAL THINKING EXERCISES

1. Go to the campus library and find a comprehensive list of voter registration laws in all 50 states. Compare this list with voter turnout in the states in the 1988 and 1992 presidential elections (the reference librarian can assist you very easily; you may wish to consult *Congressional Quarterly Weekly Report* on your own accord). How does voter turnout in your home state compare with that in the rest of the country? How might you explain the differences?

2. Ask your family members and peers the following questions: "Generally speaking, do you usually think of yourself as a Republican, Democrat, an Independent, or what?" If the respondent answers "Democrat" or "Republican," the next question is: "Would you call yourself a strong Democrat [Republican] or not so strong Democrat [Republican]?" If the respondent answers "Independent," he or she is asked: "Do you think of yourself as closer to the Republican party or the Democratic party?" Tally the total number of responses. Compare your results with those in Table 7.2 (for 1994). Would you expect similar results? Why or why not?

3. You have been named campaign manager for a local candidate running for state senate. What strategies will you employ in your campaign? How will you get your candidate elected? What factors will be stressed in your campaign?

ANSWERS TO THE PRACTICE EXAM

1.	D	11.	D
2.	D	12.	A
3.	C	13.	D
4.	A	14.	D
5.	B	15.	C
6.	A	16.	C
7.	D	17.	A
8.	A	18.	B
9.	C	19.	D
10.	C	20.	C

21. People who vote, similar to those who are knowledgeable about politics, tend to have distinct socioeconomic, demographic, and psychological characteristics. The most important variable for explaining turnout is socioeconomic: education. People with more formal schooling tend to vote at higher levels. The other important socioeconomic variable is family income and occupational status. Those with more money are drawn into social circles of people who are most interested in politics. Demographic factors also have a significant bearing on voter turnout. Among these are race and ethnicity, age, and gender. Non-Hispanic whites vote at the highest levels, while African-Americans, Hispanics, and Asians vote at lower rates. Bear in mind, however, that within each group education and income are key contributing factors influencing turnout. Age is important as well. Middle-aged Americans vote in the highest proportions, because they perceive they have the most to win or lose in politics. Youthful Americans vote in the lowest proportions, as they tend to be more interested in non-political entities. Gender is important primarily in a historical sense. Women used to vote in extremely low proportions after given franchise. But now women at least vote at the same rate as men, and in some cases higher. Several psychological characteristics and attitudes also contribute to voter turnout, including party identification, sense of efficacy (the feeling that one can have an effect on politics), and group consciousness (one's identification with a social group). Lastly, people who are interested in politics and who follow current events in the print media are also more likely to follow politics than those who are not interested and who do not follow politics in the print media. Those who read about politics learn a lot more than those who only watch television.

22. State registration laws can affect voter turnout a great deal. By the manipulation of voting laws, legislators can influence how many people, and also which people, vote. These rules can therefore have a major impact on public policies set by the government and who wins political conflicts. Registering to vote still remains a major obstacle to voting for many Americans. In states with lenient registration laws (e.g., Election Day registration), voting participation is high. In states with tougher laws, participation is lower. The most important aspect of state laws governing registration is the closing date, or the last day when one must register in order to be eligible to vote in the upcoming election. States that allow Election Day registration typically have higher turnout than those that close off registration thirty days before the election. Southern states have amongst the toughest voter registration laws in the country. Discouraging people to vote is a legacy that dates back to the post-Civil War era to disenfranchise blacks and reduce the power of poor whites.

23. Since 1896, voter turnout has been declining from 85 percent to just over 50 percent today. The decline is puzzling because of the rising level of education since the turn of the century, and the easing of voter registration laws since the 1960s. Two competing theories have been offered to explain the decrease since 1896. One theory put forth contends that both parties have put forth corporate-conservative platforms since 1896, which offers little to the working class. Many people since this time have dropped out of politics and stopped voting. Another theory is based on the premise that turnout declined not because the parties shifted toward business interests but because of changes in voting laws. These theorists focus on three changes in voting laws: the introduction of the Australian ballot (1889-1896), the passage of laws requiring people to register to vote (1890-1920), and the passage of the Nineteenth Amendment (1920). Australian ballots

allowed people to vote in private for the first time. The printing of ballots was taken away from the political parties. Party bosses could no longer force people to go to the polls and vote for them. The passage of registration laws meant that people could no longer show up on Election Day and vote. The Nineteenth Amendment gave women the right to vote, a right that many women did not exercise for decades due to the fact that women were socialized to believe that politics was men's business.

24. Many factors influence candidate selections by the voters. The most important, however, are party identification, candidate characteristics, and issues. Of these, party identification is the most crucial. People identify with political parties in the same way they identify with religions or ethnicities. Party identification is a way in which people think of themselves and is an influence on how they behave. People who think of themselves as Democrats tend to vote for Democratic candidates, while those who think of themselves as Republicans generally support Republican candidates. Candidates' personalities, experiences, past records, and even their physical appearances make up another set of voting influences called candidate characteristics. Issues are a third important factor. Although Americans are generally lacking in knowledge about substantive issues, issues still play a role in elections. The lack of knowledge does, however, affect the type of issues that are emphasized in campaigns. Issues influence voting behavior in two ways, retrospectively and prospectively. Retrospective issue voting involves making electoral decisions based on past policy outcomes. Prospective issue voting entails deciding how to vote on the basis of what policies the candidates are likely to follow in the future. The conventional wisdom concerning retrospective voting is that people vote their pocketbooks, by rewarding or punishing incumbents for the voters' personal economic situations. Prospective issue voting tends to have a minimal influence on voting decisions, especially with complicated issues requiring some substantive knowledge.

25. Although voting patterns may change from one election to the next, most post-1930s presidential elections conform to a particular pattern. Groups favoring the Democratic Party include the poor, the poorly educated, people in union households, African Americans and Hispanics, Catholics, Jews, women, and liberals. Groups favoring the Republican Party include the wealthy, the well educated, people without union members in their families, whites, Asian Americans, white Protestants, men, and conservatives.

SUMMARY

Freedom of the press is essential to the health of any democracy. Without an investigative news media, the public would be unable to monitor the actions of the government. This public dependence on the media allows the media a great deal of leeway in influencing public opinion and government behavior. As a result, the media does have an influence on politics in the United States. This influence is minimal on the way Americans view political issues as compared to the media's substantial impact on putting issues on the political agenda. The power of the media should be put in appropriate context, however. Most of the time reporters focus on what Americans are thinking and what the government is doing.

The nature of the news business has changed dramatically since the late 1700s. Partisan journalism has given way to more objective reporting, while television has supplanted newspapers as the most common source of news. Because freedom of the press is valued highly in the United States, laws extend great freedoms to journalists. The government only exercises limited regulation over the media in the aggregate.

OUTLINE

Opening Story: 1993 Rolling Stone *Interview with President Bill Clinton*

In November of 1993, President Bill Clinton was interviewed by two reporters from *Rolling Stone*. In this interview, he denounced the news media as a "knee-jerk liberal press." Bill Clinton was certainly not the first president to criticize the press for being unfair and inaccurate, as similar accounts can be traced to the early years of the republic. Although not new, complaints about the news media are nevertheless disturbing, as in many ways the success of a democracy rests on the existence of a free and impartial press. Without a free press, the public could not hold the government accountable for its actions, because it would have no practical mechanism for finding out what the government is doing.

Do the News Media Matter? (p. 233)

The News Media and Public Opinion (p. 233)

The News Media and the Political Agenda (p. 234)

The News Media and Government (p. 235)

The Changing Face of the News Media (p. 236)

Changes in Journalistic Conventions (p. 236)

Changes in Readership and Viewership (p. 238)

Changes in Media Ownership (p. 243)

Freedom of the Press (p. 245)

Limits to Press Freedom (p. 246)

The Electronic Media (p. 247)

Reporting the News (p. 249)

What is News? (p. 249)

Telling the Story (p. 251)

Evaluating the News Media (p. 254)

Ideological Bias (p. 254)

Cynicism (p. 256)

News as Entertainment (p. 257)

On the Campaign Trail (p. 258)

Reporting Leaks (p. 262)

The News Media and Democracy (p. 263)

Summary (p. 263)

Key Terms (p. 264)

Readings for Further Study (p. 265)

KEY TERMS, CONCEPTS, EVENTS, AND PEOPLE

Be able to identify and/or define each of the following and state its importance in a short paragraph.

Selective perception (p. 234)

Political agenda (p. 234)

Spin control (p. 235)

Yellow journalism (p. 236)

Muckraking (p. 237)

Objective press (p. 237)

Broadcast television (p. 240)

Cable television (p. 240)

Talk radio (p. 241)

Freedom of Information Act (p. 246)

Pool reporting (p. 247)

Federal Communications Commission (FCC) (p. 248)

Equal-time provision (p. 248)

Fairness doctrine (p. 248)

Pack journalism (p. 250)

Horse-race journalism (p. 258)

Photo opportunities (p. 259)

Sound bite (p. 260)

Leak (p. 262)

LEARNING OBJECTIVES

After reading chapter 8, students should be able to:

1. Explain why freedom of the press is essential to health of a democracy.
2. Discuss the influence the news media have on public opinion and government behavior, especially the news media's influence on the shape of the political agenda.
3. Trace the evolution of the news business over the past two hundred years, and be able to distinguish among the partisan press, penny press, yellow journalism, muckraking, and objective journalism.
4. Explain how the changing nature of the news business, which includes the rise of cable television, radio and television talk shows, and the Internet, illustrates the immense freedom the media have to define their role in the American political system.
5. Discuss the concentration of media ownership in the United States and its effect on news coverage.
6. Discuss the freedoms the news media have to cover the news, while at the same time noting that the "freedom of the press" is somewhat limited by formal legal checks (laws on libel, obscenity, and prior restraint) and informal checks (government secrecy, government pressure, and limited access to news stories).

7.   Name the four main areas in which the Federal Communications Commission regulates the electronic media (that is, television and radio), explain why the electronic media face government regulations that do not apply to the print press, and show why the electronic media have tremendous freedom to cover the news despite these regulations.

8.   Explain why the decision on what constitutes "news" is a subjective matter, discuss the criteria that journalists use to select specific news stories, and describe the relative attention journalists give to different kinds of stories.

9.   Explain the four rules journalists try to follow when reporting the news and discuss why even scrupulous attention to these rules does not guarantee objective or even fair reporting.

10. Discuss how the public's dependence on the news media for information about government creates a potential problem: the press may abuse its power by distorting the information it provides the public.

11. Assess the validity of the claim that the news media have a liberal-left bias.

12. Assess the validity of the claim that the news media increasingly treat news as entertainment.

13. Describe the common criticisms of how the news media covered the 1988 presidential election campaign and discuss the success that journalists had in trying to improve their coverage of the 1992 presidential campaign.

14. Discuss the rise of radio and television talk-shows and assess the competing claims about whether they show democracy at its best or at its worst.

15. Explain the role that leaks play in American politics and assess complaints that the news media's willingness to report stories on the basis of leaks threatens the democratic process in the United States.

PRACTICE EXAM

(Answers appear at the end of this chapter)

Multiple Choice

1.   The term news media
     a.   was invented by the Framers of the Constitution.
     b.   was invented in the latter part of the eighteenth century to describe newspaper reporters.
     c.   was invented during the Civil War to describe reporters sympathetic to the Union forces.
     d.   was invented in the twentieth century to describe radio and television reporters.

2.   The news media play a major role in shaping
     a.   the political agenda.
     b.   public policy making.
     c.   public opinion.
     d.   the outcome of elections.

3.   Which of the following has the GREATEST impact on what the public thinks?
     a.   newspapers
     b.   radio
     c.   television
     d.   *Time* magazine

4.   Which of the following attempts to use the practice of spin control?
     a.   The president
     b.   Members of Congress
     c.   Members of the executive branch
     d.   All of the above

5.   Newspapers during Thomas Jefferson's era
     a.   were heavily partisan.
     b.   were only affordable to the wealthy.
     c.   were dependent upon business and political groups.
     d.   All of the above.

6.   The penny press
     a.   began during the 1920s.
     b.   revolutionized journalism.
     c.   was dependent upon the political parties for money.
     d.   None of the above.

7.   The rise of yellow journalism occurred
     a.   during the 1830s.
     b.   during the 1890s.
     c.   during the Civil Rights movement.
     d.   during the presidential election of 1988.

8. Objectivity emerged as the touchstone of American journalism
   a. after the Revolutionary War.
   b. after the Civil War.
   c. after World War I.
   d. after World War II.

9. Muckrakers viewed their job as
   a. printing sensational news stories about famous people.
   b. exposing injustices in society.
   c. criticizing the president of the United States.
   d. increasing the circulation of newspapers in their respective cities.

10. Where do Americans get most of their news?
    a. television
    b. newspapers
    c. radio
    d. magazines

11. Who is responsible for starting a twenty-four-hour all-news cable channel?
    a. Joseph Pulitzer
    b. William Randolph Hearst
    c. Ted Turner
    d. Peter Jennings

12. The most influential news organizations in the United States are typically owned by
    a. small companies.
    b. families.
    c. large corporations.
    d. None of the above.

13. What is the most common legal check on the media?
    a. prior restraint
    b. libel laws
    c. obscenity laws
    d. public opinion

14. The FCC is
    a. controlled by Congress.
    b. controlled by the president.
    c. an independent federal regulatory agency.
    d. controlled typically by radicals.

15. The equal-time provision
    a. helps to provide "reasonable opportunities for the expression of opposing views on controversial issues of public importance."
    b. was struck down by the Supreme Court.
    c. is not necessary because all campaigns are funded equally.
    d. ensures that all candidates for public office have access to the airwaves under the same conditions.

16. Journalists tend to
    a. gravitate toward conflict.
    b. cover the failures of government rather than its successes.
    c. cover stories that are likely to affect the lives of their audience.
    d. All of the above.

17. In news reporting, which of the following statements concerning bias is MOST accurate?
    a. National journalists have a definite liberal bias.
    b. National journalists have a definite conservative bias.
    c. The media tends to treat news as entertainment.
    d. National journalists have a bias against Republican presidents.

18. In the 1988 presidential election, the media
    a. spent too much time on horse-race journalism.
    b. were not manipulated by the candidates.
    c. did a good job at covering the issues.
    d. would not allow Ross Perot equal time with George Bush and Michael Dukakis.

19. What is a significant ramification of the shrinking sound bite?
    a. Americans know more about public affairs.
    b. Americans know more about where each presidential candidate stands on the issues.
    c. Americans seldom hear presidential candidates speak at length about their views.
    d. None of the above.

20. Which of the following stories was NOT the product of a leak?
    a. Watergate affair
    b. Allegations of sexual harassment against Clarence Thomas
    c. Both a + b
    d. None of the above.

Essays

21.   How does the news media influence American politics? In your response, be sure to include a discussion of the role of the media in a democracy, and with regards to public opinion, the political agenda, and the government.
22.   Discuss the changes in journalistic conventions from the beginning of the republic to the present.
23.   Explain the ways in which the electronic media are regulated. Which governmental agency is responsible for the regulations? Do the same rules apply to the print media? Why or why not?
24.   What criteria do journalists utilize when deciding what is news? Explain.
25.   Respond to the following assertion: The national media have a liberal bias. Do you agree or disagree? Be sure to explain why or why not.

CRITICAL THINKING EXERCISES

1.   Assemble into groups of three. Watch one of the following television nightly news broadcasts: ABC, NBC, and CBS. Have your two peers watch the other stations. Compile a chronological list of all stories covered and compare them with your peers. Using the categories in Table 8.2, compare your percentages. How are they similar?
2.   Get a copy of *Citizen Kane* and view it. What lessons can be learned from this classic movie?
3.   Tom Brokaw argues that "Bias, like beauty, is most often in the eye of the beholder." Write a critical analysis of his perspective on bias in the media.

ANSWERS TO THE PRACTICE EXAM

1.	D	11.	C
2.	A	12.	C
3.	C	13.	B
4.	D	14.	C
5.	D	15.	D
6.	B	16.	D
7.	B	17.	C
8.	C	18.	A
9.	B	19.	C
10.	A	20.	C

21.   The media has a significant, though complex, influence on American politics. While the media does not have the power to dictate fundamental beliefs, the influence that it has sustained raises anxieties about the media's role in a democracy. The Framers of the Constitution believed that democracy could not flourish without a free press. In their view, the press was essential to hold the government accountable by the people. While most Americans believe that the media exerts considerable influence over public opinion, research suggests that news coverage has at most only a modest effect on public opinion. This is undoubtedly due to the fact that people utilize their own pre-existing beliefs about the world to make sense of what they come across in the media. Even though the media does not have a significant impact on what Americans think, the various media sources (especially television) have considerable influence over what Americans think about. Researchers have discovered that the media plays a large role in shaping the political agenda. Bear in mind, however, that research has indicated that the media does not consciously or maliciously attempt to manipulate the political agenda. Finally, similar to public opinion and the political agenda, the media does at times influence what government does and does not do. Yet since news coverage has the potential to influence both public opinion and the political agenda, government officials actively attempt to influence news coverage (e.g., spin control). Thus the role of the media in American politics is very complex.

22. Journalistic conventions have changed dramatically since Thomas Jefferson's era. In the early 1800s, the newspapers were a partisan press, meaning that they had formal ties to political parties or other political groups. At that time, the high cost of paper confined circulation only to the wealthy. During the partisan press, the link between party and press accounts was very strong. The penny press evolved in the 1830s. This revolutionized journalism because it relied on mass circulation to succeed. As a result, more Americans became literate. Although the penny press did not have formal ties to the parties, newspapers often took up issues that favored one candidate or another, but political influence was not its purpose. Yellow journalism became popular in the 1890s, where sensational and lurid stories often supplanted concrete news. The turn of the century also witnessed an investigative type of reporting called muckraking. Muckrakers viewed their job as exposing wrongdoing by the government. Similar to the yellow journalists, muckrakers were often not very objective in their reporting. Following World War I, a new convention came about that is still utilized today: the objective press. This form of journalism stresses the need for journalists to keep their opinion out of their coverage of the news.

23. The electronic media must contend with numerous regulations that are not applicable to the print media. The additional constraints on the electronic media are necessary for two reasons. First, the scarcity argument dictates that the number of channels is limited, so the competition is more limited. Second, the airwaves belong to the people and not to any single individual or group, so more government control may be warranted. The agency that oversees the electronic media is the FCC (Federal Communications Commission), an independent federal agency that regulations the television and radio industries. The FCC has four main tasks. First, it administers the rules on cross-ownership. Second, it sets technical standards for the communications industry. A third task is the licensing of tv and radio stations to use the public airwaves. Lastly, the FCC also sets and administers broadcast standards, such as the equal-time provision, for example.

24. What constitutes news is obviously very subjective. There are many events around the world that could be covered. In selecting what is newsworthy, journalists are typically governed by three important criteria. The first is conflict. Conflict is a primary focus because journalists view their job as sifting out bad news, and this helps to explain why the media tends to focus on the failures of government rather than the successes. A second factor is proximity. Media members often select stories that are salient to the lives of their audience. A final key factor is timeliness. Journalists like to cover the new and unusual.

25. Most Americans contend that the media have a liberal bias. Some utilize survey research (the fact that journalists are far more likely to be liberal than does the public) to substantiate their claims. Yet surveys say nothing about what journalists actually write in performing their jobs. There may be a considerable gap between personal opinions and news coverage. There are other factors that contradict this prevalent belief. Journalism is a team effort. Most of what is reported is the product of many people collaborating. Journalists must also report to corporate executives, who tend to be conservative. These executives tend to hire reporters who avoid advocacy. Survey research, therefore, cannot help scholars ascertain whether or not the media have a particular type of bias. Analysis of various presidential elections should also be scrutinized carefully. Examples of unfair reporting can always be found. As a result, it would be unwise to accuse the media of having a liberal bias at this time. The research to date has not been conclusive.

SUMMARY

Political parties evolved for practical reasons. Politicians wanted the parties to assist them in winning elections so that they could in turn pursue public policy goals. They perform a vital function in a democracy, as parties help to make elected officials accountable for their actions. Unlike many other democracies, the U.S. has a two-party system in which both parties can be described as centrist. According to the spatial theory of elections, politicians in single-member, plurality electoral systems such as the United States are more likely to win elections if they join into two large, centrist parties. Although parties have changed a great deal in U.S. history, they still seek to win elections and thus still serve as links helping voters hold politicians accountable.

OUTLINE

Opening Story: Political Parties and American Elections

Every time there is a presidential election, there is more at stake than simply the presidency. Candidates representing the two major political parties contend for many important elected offices in the United States. Even though Bill Clinton was declared the victor early in the evening on Election Day in 1996, he remained quite interested in the election results of many other offices, especially elections in the U.S. House of Representatives and the U.S. Senate. In this regard, political parties can be viewed as "teams."

Although parties were not envisioned by the Framers of the Constitution, they evolved quickly because of conflict. They were created by politicians to help them with their goals, including winning elections and making public policy.

What is a Political Party? (p. 268)

Party Functions (p. 269)

Characteristics of U.S. Political Parties (p. 271)

The Spatial Theory of Elections (p. 272)

The U.S. Two-Party System vs. Multiparty Systems (p. 275)

The Spatial Model Applied to Real Politics (p. 276)

The History of U.S. Parties and Elections (p. 279)

The First Party System (1796-1824) (p. 279)

The Second Party System (1828-1856) (p. 279)

The Third Party System (1860-1892) (p. 280)

The Fourth Party System (1896-1928) (p. 280)

The Fifth Party System (1932-?) (p. 281)

Critical Elections and Party Realignment Theory (p. 281)

From Realignment to Dealignment? (p. 282)

The Uncertain Future (p. 283)

Modern Party Organization (p. 284)

Local Organizations (p. 285)

State Organizations (p. 290)

National Organizations (p. 291)

Relationships Among Party Organizations (p. 292)

Summary (p. 292)

Key Terms (p. 293)

Readings for Further Study (p. 293)

KEY TERMS, CONCEPTS, EVENTS, AND PEOPLE

Be able to identify and/or define each of the following and state its importance in a short paragraph.

Political party (p. 268)

Political cleavages (p. 268)

Direct primary (p. 270)

Caucus/convention system (p. 270)

Two-party system (p. 271)

Centrist parties (p. 271)

Median voter hypothesis (p. 273)

Single-member, plurality electoral system (p. 275)

Proportional representation system (p. 275)

Duverger's Law (p. 276)

Party platform (p. 276)

New Deal coalition (p. 281)

Critical elections (p. 281)

Party realignment (p. 281)

Party dealignment (p. 283)

Party machine (p. 285)

Patronage job (p. 285)

Australian ballot (p. 286)

Candidate-centered campaigns (p. 289)

LEARNING OBJECTIVES

After reading chapter 9, students should be able to:

1. Define what constitutes a political party and show that parties are organized around the basic cleavages in society.
2. Identify the seven functions that parties may perform.
3. Defend the claim that the United States has a centrist, two-party system and explain what those terms mean.
4. Explain the basic argument of the spatial theory of elections and why it generates the median voter hypothesis.
5. Explain the difference between the single-member, plurality electoral system used in the United States and the proportional representation systems used in most other democracies, and identify the consequences this difference has for political parties.
6. Identify the five party systems in American history and list the basic cleavages within each party system.
7. Define the concepts of critical elections and party realignment.
8. Discuss the competing arguments in the debate over party realignment.

9. Define the concept of party dealignment and discuss the claim that the United States has moved toward dealignment since the late 1960s.
10. Identify the hierarchy of party offices within each party, and recognize that the organizations at the top of the hierarchy do not have much control over organizations below them.
11. Define what constitutes a party machine and discuss how they survived by relying on selective, material benefits.
12. Define what constitutes the Progressive Era, identify the major political reforms it introduced, and assess its impact on party machines.
13. Define what constitutes a candidate-centered campaign and explain why they developed in most areas of the United States following the decline of strong parties.
14. Explain the role of state party organizations and identify the limits on their power.
15. Explain the role of national party organizations, identify the limits on their power, and list the range of services they currently perform.

PRACTICE EXAM

(Answers appear at the end of this chapter)

Multiple Choice

1. Closed primaries
   a. allow voters to choose on Election Day the party primary in which they will vote.
   b. permit voters to jump back and forth among the parties while they vote.
   c. require voters to indicate their party affiliations prior to Election Day.
   d. are only utilized by the Republican party.

2. The Republican party formed in
   a. 1800.
   b. 1854.
   c. 1888.
   d. 1932.

3. In the 1992 presidential election, Ross Perot can be described best as
   a. the liberal candidate.
   b. the conservative candidate.
   c. the moderate candidate.
   d. the protest candidate.

4. In proportional electoral systems,
   a. legislatures are elected at large.
   b. legislatures are divided into districts.
   c. legislatures are selected according to Duverger's Law.
   d. legislatures are selected according to the winner-take-all principle.

5. In proportional electoral systems,
   a. minor parties hardly ever exist.
   b. minor parties can prosper.
   c. minor party candidates hardly ever win seats in the national legislature.
   d. None of the above.

6. The Republican Party was originally founded as
   a. the party of big business.
   b. the party of working-class Americans.
   c. the anti-slavery party.
   d. the party of Thomas Jefferson.

7. Since civil rights legislation was passed in the 1960s,
   a. Southern whites have become more Democratic.
   b. Southern whites have become more Republican.
   c. Blacks have become more Republican.
   d. None of the above.

8. The Federalist Party
   a. was very strong until the Civil War.
   b. was supportive of a weak federal government.
   c. was founded by James Madison.
   d. did not last long.

9. Reconstruction describes
   a. the colonies after the Revolutionary War.
   b. the period during which the South was occupied by Union forces.
   c. the merging of the Federalist and Whig Parties.
   d. the New Deal era.

10. The fourth party system was dominated by the
    a. Republicans.
    b. Democrats.
    c. Whigs.
    d. Know-Nothings.

11. The last realigning election in the U.S. occurred in
    a. 1860.
    b. 1896.
    c. 1932.
    d. 1968.

12. Party machines are created by
    a. chance.
    b. the use of selective, material incentives.
    c. force.
    d. liberal politicians.

13. Which of the following DID NOT occur during the Progressive era?
    a. Spoils system
    b. Australian ballot
    c. Direct primary
    d. Merit system

14. The second party system was ushered in with the election of _____ as president.
    a. Thomas Jefferson
    b. Andrew Jackson
    c. Abraham Lincoln
    d. Henry Clay

15. Who was president during the Great Depression?
    a. Calvin Coolidge
    b. Warren Harding
    c. Herbert Hoover
    d. Franklin Delano Roosevelt

16. Who was the only Republican president during the time period 1933-1969?
    a. Gerald Ford
    b. Dwight David Eisenhower
    c. Thomas Dewey
    d. Calvin Coolidge

17. Which of the following is an accurate description of political party organizations?
    a. Power and authority are vested at the top of the party's organizational hierarchy.
    b. Parties are very strong and centralized organizations.
    c. Party organizations are loose confederations that agree to cooperate to achieve a common goal.
    d. Parties no longer have formal organizational structures.

18. Which of the following demonstrates that parties are in a period of dealignment?
    a. A higher proportion of Americans consider themselves to be strong Democrats.
    b. A higher proportion of Americans consider themselves to be strong Republicans.
    c. A higher proportion of Americans use split-ticket voting.
    d. Ross Perot received 19% of the popular vote in the 1992 presidential election.

19. Which of the following is an accurate description of political parties in the 1990s.
    a. Voters in the South and Rocky Mountain West are becoming more Republican.
    b. Voters in the Northeast and Midwest are becoming more Democratic.
    c. No one is sure whether or not a new party realignment will occur.
    d. All of the above.

20. How was the urban party machine in Chicago dismantled in the 1970s?
    a. By the death of Mayor Richard Daley.
    b. By scandals.
    c. By the efforts of reformists, including Michael Shakman and Mayor Harold Washington.
    d. By laws passed in the Illinois legislature.

Essays

21.   What are the specific functions performed by parties in a political system?

22.   Explain what is meant by the spatial theory of elections. Be sure to include a discussion of the median voter hypothesis in your response.

23.   Briefly describe the history of political parties and elections in the U.S.

24.   Many contend that the parties in America are in a period of dealignment. What does this mean? Do you agree or disagree? What evidence can you cite to substantiate your position?

25.   What were some of the reforms established during the Progressive Era and how did the changes weaken the political parties?

CRITICAL THINKING EXERCISES

1.   Using Figure 9.5, determine how strong the two major political parties are in your state. Try to ascertain why parties in other states may be stronger or weaker.

2.   According to federal law, individuals can contribute no more than $1,000 to each candidate for each election, and political action committees, or PACs, can contribute no more than $5,000. Suppose that Congress passes a new law which bans all contributions from individuals and PACs in favor of a system which funds presidential and congressional campaigns with public monies. Would such a system be an improvement over the current financing situation? How would it affect the presidential and congressional election processes?

3.   Compare the contemporary Democratic and Republican parties with the parties that formed during the first party system (1796-1824). What are the fundamental philosophical differences between the parties in both eras? Are they similar or different? How would you compare modern politicians such as Ted Kennedy and Ronald Reagan with some of the politicians of this early era such as Alexander Hamilton and Thomas Jefferson? What types of conflictual issues did each of these politicians debate?

ANSWERS TO THE PRACTICE EXAM

1.	C	11.	C
2.	B	12.	B
3.	D	13.	A
4.	A	14.	B
5.	B	15.	C
6.	C	16.	B
7.	B	17.	C
8.	D	18.	C
9.	B	19.	D
10.	A	20.	C

21.   Political parties perform many functions in the political system. First, parties recruit candidates for office. Second, parties nominate candidates through primaries, caucuses, conventions, and other means. Third, parties help to mobilize voters through party identification. Fourth, parties contest elections. This can be considered the core function of parties. Fifth, parties form governments. Once elected, officials organize governments around party lines. Sixth, parties coordinate policy across independent units of government. Since few problems can be dealt with effectively by one branch of government, party loyalties can often provide the basis for building coalitions needed to make public policies. Seventh, parties provide accountability. Party labels help voters to identify with whom they wish to either reward or punish.

22.   The spatial theory of elections is helpful in understanding why both major parties in the United States are centrist. According to proponents of this theory, politicians in the United States are more likely to achieve their goals if they join one of the two centrist parties (Democrats and Republicans). The "real" world is simplified by creating a single scale for all political issues. The scale ranges from 0 (liberal) to 100 (conservative). The midpoint, 50, reflects the political center. The median voter hypothesis postulates that this midpoint is the best possible position for a politician who only cares about winning elections, because the center is the most appealing place for most voters. The candidate who is closest to the median should win any given election.

23.   The history of parties and elections in the United States is often divided into five periods by historians. The first party system occurred from 1796-1824. This was a period where Thomas Jefferson's Democratic-Republican party dominated over Alexander Hamilton's Federalists. The second party system occurred from 1828, when Andrew Jackson's Democratic Party came to power, to 1856. The opposition party was the Whigs. The third party system covered the era 1860-1892. Abraham Lincoln's Republican Party dominated over the Democrats. The fourth party system ran from 1896-1928. The Republican Party again dominated over the Democrats, yet the party had evolved from one of abolitionism to one that supported the interests of big business. The fifth party system began in 1932 and, according to many analysts, has not run its course. The dominant party during the first part of this era was the Democratic Party of Franklin Delano Roosevelt (New Deal Democrats). Since the 1960s, however, both major parties have witnessed successes in elections at least in part. Republicans have been successful at capturing the presidency, while Democrats have done well in congressional elections.

24.   Many scholars believe that the two major political parties in the United States are in a period of dealignment. Party dealignment is a trend toward weakening voter loyalties to both major parties. Based on the data available, the increases in split-ticket voting and the number of people identifying themselves as independents indicates that party labels matter less to people than they did in the past. Such evidence would help to substantiate the assertion that parties are currently undergoing a period of dealignment.

25.   Many reforms were established during the Progressive Era (1890-1920). Some of the major changes included the introduction of the Australian ballot, the implementation of the direct primary, and the spread of the merit system. All of these changes had a profound impact on the strength of political parties. With the introduction of the Australian ballot, people could vote secretly for the first time. Before, people got their ballots from the local party and therefore had to vote in full view of local party officials. The local parties could reward supporters and punish those who did not. The Australian ballot ended this system and forced parties to focus on persuading voters rather than threatening them. The advent of the direct primary also weakened the parties. Under the old system, party bosses selected their own candidates to field in general elections. With the direct primary, party bosses lost not only the ability to nominate candidates, but also the ability to influence the behavior of elected officials as well. Political power was therefore transferred from the local party organizations to elected officials. A third reform was the spread of the civil service system (often called the merit system). Under the old spoils system, city and county employees were hired for political reasons. If they became disloyal, party bosses could fire them. Under the merit system, government employees were hired on the basis of merit alone, and were protected from being fired on the basis of politics. As a result, many urban party machines dismantled.

Chapter 10   Interest Groups

SUMMARY

The primary function of interest groups is to influence policy-making by the government. They have always been an integral part of American politics, as Alexis de Tocqueville's account of interest groups in the early nineteenth century documents. Since the number of interest groups has increased dramatically in recent years, more Americans are concerned that policy-making by the government is less a product of the public's preferences, and more of a reflection of interest group politics. While it is clear that there is a definitive bias in interest group representation in favor of the affluent and well educated, it is also true that interest group politics can be very pluralistic as well.

OUTLINE

Opening Story: Interest Groups and the Proposed Rewriting of the Nation's Law on Mining on Federal Lands

In 1993, officials in the Clinton Administration proposed rewriting the nation's law on mining on federal lands. The existing law was passed in 1872, when attracting settlers to the West was more important than protecting the federal treasury or the environment. This law allowed miners to buy public land for as little as $2.50 an acre, and posed no taxes on the gold, silver, or other minerals that they extracted. Environmental groups applauded the Administration's proposal; mining companies denounced it. They argued that it would drive up the cost of mining, force them to fire thousands of workers, and doom many mining communities in the West. Under pressure from mining companies and their employees, members of Congress from mining states opposed the administration's plan. The plan was defeated after two years of legislative wrangling.

        The defeat of this proposal demonstrates the potential influence that interest groups can have on public policy making in the United States. In *Federalist Number 10*, James Madison warned that factions (interest groups) could harm the public good. Americans today are still concerned that government officials are beholden to special interest groups. This issue illustrates a fundamental question in American politics: do interest groups help or harm democracy?

Defining Interest Groups (p. 296)

Interest Groups versus Political Parties (p. 297)

The Roles of Interest Groups (p. 297)

The Growth of Interest Groups (p. 299)

The Diversity of Organized Interests (p. 300)

Economic Interest Groups (p. 300)

Citizen Groups (p. 301)

Government Interest Groups (p. 302)

Coalitions and Divisions (p. 303)

Interest Group Formation and Maintenance (p. 304)

Obstacles to Interest Group Formation (p. 304)

Overcoming Obstacles to Interest Group Formation (p. 305)

Interest Group Maintenance (p. 307)

Interest Group Bias (p. 307)

Interest Group Strategies (p. 308)

Creating Political Action Committees (p. 308)

Lobbying the Government (p. 312)

Mobilizing Public Opinion (p. 316)

Litigating (p. 320)

Interest Group Influence (p. 320)

External Factors (p. 321)

Internal Factors (p. 322)

The Balance Sheet on Interest Groups (p. 323)

A Love/Hate Relationship (p. 323)

Calls for Reform (p. 325)

The Contributions of Interest Groups (p. 327)

Summary (p. 327)

Key Terms (p. 328)

Readings for Further Study (p. 328)

KEY TERMS, CONCEPTS, EVENTS, AND PEOPLE

Be able to identify and/or define each of the following and state its importance in a short paragraph.

Interest Group (p. 296)

Citizen Groups (p. 301)

Disturbance theory (p. 305)

Collective goods dilemma (p. 305)

Free riders (p. 305)

Material benefits (p. 306)

Solidary benefits (p. 306)

Expressive benefits (p. 306)

Selective benefits (p. 306)

Political action committees (PACs) (p. 308)

Lobbying (p. 312)

Lobbyists (p. 313)

Direct lobbying (p. 313)

Advocacy advertising (p. 316)

Grass-roots lobbying (p. 317)

Astroturf lobbying (p. 319)

Amicus curiae brief (p. 320)

LEARNING OBJECTIVES

After reading chapter 10, students should be able to:

1. Define what an interest group is and explain how it differs from a political party.
2. Explain the five main functions that interest groups perform: representation, participation, education, agenda building, and program monitoring.
3. Discuss how interest groups have been a feature of American politics since the inception of the Republic and explain why the number of interest groups has grown tremendously over the last several decades.
4. Describe the tremendous diversity of organized interest groups and explain the different objectives of the three main categories of interest groups, economic interest groups, citizen groups and government interest groups.
5. Explain that some interest groups form for reasons having nothing to do with politics and become involved in interest group politics only because their interests are affected by government policy, while other interest groups form specifically for the purpose of influencing government policy.

6.   Explain how disturbance theory accounts for the formation of some interest groups.
7.   Explain why the collective goods dilemma can prevent interest groups from forming and discuss how interest groups can overcome the collective goods dilemma through entrepreneurial leadership and by providing selective benefits to their members.
8.   Discuss why the affluent and better educated are more likely to belong to interest groups than are the poor and less educated.
9.   Discuss the four main strategies that interest groups use to influence government policy: creating a political action committee, lobbying government officials, mobilizing public opinion, and litigating.
10. Discuss the rise of political action committees (PACs) in American politics and assess the validity of claims that PACs enable interest groups to buy votes in Congress.
11. Explain what direct lobbying is and discuss what lobbyists do to influence government policy.
12. Explain why interest groups sometimes seek to mobilize public opinion and describe the three main strategies that interest groups use to mobilize public opinion, education campaigns, grass-roots lobbying, and political protests.
13. Explain how interest groups try to influence government policy by going to court.
14. Discuss the external and internal factors that affect the ability of an interest group to influence government policy.
15. Assess the impact that interest groups have on American politics and discuss the potential problems raised by proposals to restrict interest group activity.

PRACTICE EXAM

(Answers appear at the end of this chapter)

Multiple Choice

1. Who said that "Americans of all ages, all stations in life, and all types of disposition, are forever forming associations."
    a.   Alexis de Tocqueville
    b.   King George III
    c.   Abraham Lincoln
    d.   Ross Perot

2. Interest groups
    a.   began to organize over the slavery issue.
    b.   began to organize in the early 1900s.
    c.   began to organize in the 1960s during the New Politics Movement.
    d.   have always been an integral part of American politics.

3. Which type of interest group is most common?
    a.   Organized labor
    b.   Business
    c.   Agriculture
    d.   Professional associations

4. Which of the following accounts for the rapid growth in the number of interest groups.
    a.   The legacy of the 1960s
    b.   Improvements in technology
    c.   Rise of new issues
    d.   All of the above

5. Which of the following is considered to be a radical environmental interest group?
    a.   Sierra Club
    b.   Nature Conservancy
    c.   Greenpeace
    d.   National Audubon Society

6. Most people join interest groups for
    a.   material benefits.
    b.   solidary benefits.
    c.   expressive benefits.
    d.   None of the above.

7. Political action committees tend to favor
    a. Republicans.
    b. Democrats.
    c. Independents.
    d. incumbents.

8. Political action committees are limited to giving no more than _____ per election to any candidate seeking federal office.
    a. $1,000
    b. $5,000
    c. $25,000
    d. $100,000

9. The number of political action committees has
    a. increased dramatically since the 1980s.
    b. decreased dramatically since the 1980s.
    c. leveled off since the 1980s to about 4,000.
    d. leveled off since the 1980s to about 44,000.

10. Which type of political action committee spends the most money?
    a. Trade, Member, and Health PACs
    b. Labor PACs
    c. Corporate PACs
    d. Nonconnected PACs

11. What is the main tool that interest groups use in their lobbying efforts?
    a. information
    b. money
    c. threats
    d. None of the above

12. Which type of lobbying technique was used frequently by Ross Perot supporters in the 1992 presidential election?
    a. Letter-writing
    b. Phone campaigns
    c. Radio shows
    d. Petition drives

13. Which of the following interest groups uses civil disobedience as a favored tactic?
    a. Chamber of Commerce
    b. Operation Rescue
    c. League of Women's Voters
    d. Children's Defense Fund

14. *Amicus curiae* briefs are most commonly filed in lawsuits involving
    a. taxation.
    b. punitive damages.
    c. civil liberties and civil rights.
    d. health care regulations.

15. Most interest groups focus on
    a. forming PACs.
    b. lobbying the government.
    c. mobilizing public opinion.
    d. a variety of tactics in order to influence public policy.

16. College students
    a. have a lot of power in Washington, D.C.
    b. are very well organized and committed to many social issues.
    c. have very little power in Washington, D.C.
    d. None of the above.

17. Interest groups find it easier to
    a. lobby for new policies.
    b. block changes in existing policies.
    c. support policies that have a broad impact on society.
    d. influence Supreme Court justices than U.S. senators.

18. Interest groups have a strong
    a. upper class bias.
    b. working class bias.
    c. bias in favor of racial minorities.
    d. bias in favor of welfare recipients.

19. Interest groups
    a. play a vital role in democracies.
    b. are too powerful and should be strictly regulated by the government.
    c. do not allow citizens access to the government.
    d. do not allow citizens to communicate their values and expectations.

20. The success of interest groups depends upon
    a. external factors.
    b. internal factors.
    c. Both a + b.
    d. None of the above.

21.   Identify and explain the five primary functions of interest groups.
22.   Identify and explain the three main categories of interest groups.
23.   How do interest groups influence policy? Be sure to discuss four distinct categories in your response.
24.   What four internal factors affect the success of interest groups? Explain.
25.   Many Americans believe that some special interest groups are too powerful. As a result, should interest groups be limited in their ability to influence governmental policy making? Why or why not?

CRITICAL THINKING EXERCISES

1.   Find out some interest group ratings (liberal and conservative) for your representative in the U.S. House of Representatives and for your two U.S. senators (use Figure 10.4 of the text as a guide). A good source to consult is *The Almanac of American Politics*. After doing so, explain what you may have learned about your representative and senators that you did not know before the exercise.
2.   In *Federalist Number 10*, James Madison explained that factions (interest groups) can harm the public good if left unchecked. Read (or reread) this important document, and explain what practical checks exist to counteract the negative effects of interest groups on policy making by the government.
3.   Select three issues that are most important to you. What interest groups wield influence in these issues? Which ones are "good" and which ones are "bad" in your judgment? Why?

ANSWERS TO THE PRACTICE EXAM

1.	A	11.	A
2.	D	12.	D
3.	B	13.	B
4.	D	14.	C
5.	C	15.	D
6.	A	16.	C
7.	D	17.	B
8.	B	18.	A
9.	C	19.	A
10.	C	20.	C

21.   Interest groups wield influence by performing five primary functions. First, interest groups represent the interests of their members to the government. At the national level, the federal government has the power to set rules that govern nearly all aspects of society. As a result, most major interest groups have an active presence in Washington, D.C. Second, interest groups enable common people to participate in politics. For most Americans, interest group membership is a convenient and time-efficient way to influence public policy making. Third, interest groups educate the general public and government officials about issues. Oftentimes, this entails attempting to shape public opinion in order to influence policy making. Fourth, through the education process, interest groups help to push new issues on the political agenda. Fifth, interest groups monitor how the federal government administers programs. This is important, because interest group officials are not only interested in what laws are passed, but how they are actually implemented after they have been created.

22.   The three main categories of interest groups are economic interest groups, citizen (public interest) groups, and government interest groups. Economic interest groups work to advance the economic interests of their members. This includes the vast majority of all interest groups. The four main types of economic interest groups are business groups, labor unions, agricultural organizations, and professional associations. The civil

rights and anti-war movements of the 1960s spurred the rise of citizen (or public interest groups). Unlike economic interest groups, citizen groups promote their own visions of the greater public good as opposed to their own economic self-interests. Since the federal government funds and regulates many of the programs run by state and local governments, the latter two have their own interest groups to represent their causes before the government. Foreign governments also have vested interest groups for the same purpose.

23. Interest groups attempt to influence policy in four distinct ways: creating political action committees, lobbying government officials, mobilizing public opinion, and litigating. Political action committees (PACs) are organizations that solicit contributions from members of interest groups and channel the funds to election campaigns. A more direct way for trying to influence government officials is to conduct lobbying. This is a direct attempt at influencing public policy making, as many contact government officials in person. A third way to influence public policy is to mobilize public opinion. Besides lobbying, interest groups may attempt to influence policy by mobilizing public opinion in support of the group's policies. This can be accomplished through external means: education campaigns, grass-roots lobbying, and political protests. Interest groups can also influence public policy through litigation. Sometimes groups challenge the constitutionality of existing laws, at other times groups seek to force the government to enforce the existing laws properly.

24. Political scientists have created four internal factors that affect the success of interest groups: the size of the group's membership, the political skills of its leaders, its financial resources, and its objectives. In terms of interest group membership, governmental leaders are most likely to listen to interest groups with a large comparative membership. Second, skillful leadership is important to the success of any interest group. Group leaders must have a good understanding of the political process and how to represent their interests before the government. They must also know how to manage their own organizations. Third, money is an important variable in interest group politics. A large treasury enables certain interest groups to conduct more activities in their quest to influence policy, though money does not, in and of itself, guarantee success in this objective. Fourth, what the members of an interest group strive to accomplish also affects its ability to influence public policy. As a general rule, interest groups find it easier to block changes in policy than to lobby for new policies altogether.

25. While many Americans are concerned about the power of certain interest groups in their democracy, they nevertheless play a vital role in American politics. Interest groups help represent the diverse interests of the public before the government, thereby giving the people an indirect voice in policy making. They also help to educate people about the issues, push new items on the political agenda, and help the people to hold the government accountable by monitoring its activities. They also enable people to participate in politics. Limiting the freedom of interest groups to petition the government would be detrimental to the democratic process. Without interest groups, most people would have no access to the federal government and no practical manner in which to communicate their values, beliefs, and expectations.

SUMMARY

The Framers created Congress in Article I of the Constitution. This is important, because the framers intended and perceived that Congress would be the dominant branch of government in terms of policy making. To them, Congress would act as the voice of the people in the new republican form of government. The House and the Senate were made equals in lawmaking, but the framers ensured that members of the House would be more sensitive to public opinion by giving them two-year terms while shielding senators to a certain extent by giving them six-year terms. Although the basic structure of Congress is delineated in the Constitution, the House and Senate have the authority to govern their daily operations by establishing a series of rules. Because of their different sizes and traditions, both chambers operate quite unlike the other.

OUTLINE

Opening Story: Congressional Reaction to President Bill Clinton's Plan to Raise the Minimum Wage

In February of 1995, President Bill Clinton proposed to raise the minimum wage from $4.25 to $5.15 per hour. The president's plan was well received by the American public as almost 80% of the people supported it. But the Republican leaders in the Congress opposed it, fearing that it would hurt small businesses and reduce job opportunities. Without the support and interest of the members of the majority party in Congress, the president's proposal did not become enacted into law at that time. This failure illustrates that in a system of separation of powers, Congress plays an integral role in influencing and formulating policy making in the United States.

The Structure of Congress (p. 332)

Bicameralism (p. 332)

The House of Representatives (p. 333)

The Senate (p. 334)

The Evolution of Congress (p. 334)

Changing Attitudes Toward Service in Congress (p. 335)

Change in the House (p. 337)

Change in the Senate (p. 340)

Getting There and Staying There—Congressional Elections (p. 341)

Incumbents and Reelection (p. 341)

The Election Setting (p. 342)

The Incumbents' Advantages (p. 346)

The Challengers' Disadvantages (p. 351)

Voters and Election Outcomes (p. 352)

Serving in Congress (p. 353)

Who Serves? (p. 353)

Congress as a Job (p. 355)

Congress and Ethics (p. 358)

Congress as an Organization (p. 360)

Political Parties in Congress (p. 360)

Party Leadership in Congress (p. 361)

Committees (p. 364)

Staff (p. 367)

The Business of Congress (p. 367)

The Legislative Process (p. 368)

Decision Making (p. 372)

Policy Oversight (p. 376)

Congress and the Idea of Representation (p. 377)

Summary (p. 378)

Key Terms (p. 379)

Readings for Further Study (p. 380)

KEY TERMS, CONCEPTS, EVENTS, AND PEOPLE

Be able to identify and/or define each of the following and state its importance in a short paragraph.

Bicameral legislature (p. 332)

Turnover (p. 333)

Reapportionment (p. 334)

Standing committee (p. 337)

Seniority rule (p. 338)

Subcommittees (p. 338)

Caucus (p. 339)

Single-member districts (p. 342)

Gerrymandering (p. 344)

Home style (p. 346)

Constituent service (p. 347)

Franking privilege (p. 347)

Midterm elections (p. 352)

Divided government (p. 353)

Conservative Coalition (p. 363)

Conference committee (p. 365)

Select committees (p. 365)

Filibuster (p. 371)

Cloture (p. 371)

Policy oversight (p. 376)

Police-patrol oversight (p. 376)

Fire-alarm oversight (p. 377)

LEARNING OBJECTIVES

After reading chapter 11, students should be able to:

1. Identify the rules governing Congress that are set forth in the Constitution, including the rules specifying the bicameral structure of Congress, how members are selected, and the role of reapportionment in the House of Representatives.
2. Outline the political history of the House of Representatives, including the rise of careerism in the late nineteenth century, the fall of powerful speakers and the rise of the seniority rule in the early twentieth century, and the revolt of the subcommittees and decentralization of power in the 1970s.
3. Outline the modest political changes in the operation of the Senate over the past two hundred years and explain the decline of the apprenticeship system since the 1960s.
4. Explain why the House and Senate experience substantial turnover even though incumbents enjoy high reelection rates.
5. Define what redistricting and gerrymandering are, discuss what roles they play in the high rate of incumbency reelection, and assess how they relate to the question of what constitutes "fair" representation for a group.
6. Defend the claim that senators have a harder time winning reelection than representatives because most states are more diverse than congressional districts.
7. Explain how the advantages of incumbency help incumbents win reelection.
8. Explain why challengers in House and Senate elections often are at a disadvantage when compared to incumbents.
9. Explain why it is that some incumbents lose their bids for reelection despite the advantages they have over their challengers.
10. Define what "divided government" is, argue that it has become more common in recent years, and explain what its likely causes are.
11. Recognize that white males overwhelmingly dominate the membership of Congress, but that descriptive representation does not necessarily guarantee policy representation.
12. Describe the party leadership system in the House and the Senate.
13. Describe the powers of the Speaker and Minority Leader of the House of Representatives, and the limits of their power.
14. Explain the differences between the power of party leaders in the House and party leaders in the Senate.
15. Explain the committee system in the House and Senate and discuss the differences between them.
16. Explain the process by which a bill becomes law.
17. Explain how members of Congress decide how to vote when an issue comes to the floor.
18. Define what policy oversight is and explain the difference between the police-patrol and fire-alarm strategies of oversight.

PRACTICE EXAM

(Answers appear at the end of this chapter)

Multiple Choice

1. Reapportionment occurs
   a. whenever the president deems it necessary.
   b. whenever Congress deems it necessary.
   c. every ten years following the census.
   d. whenever the Supreme Court deems it necessary.

2. All tax bills
   a. must be proposed by the president.
   b. must originate in the House of Representatives.
   c. must originate in the Senate.
   d. must be approved by a public referendum.

3. According to the U.S. Constitution, senators must be at least
   a. 25 years old.
   b. 30 years old.
   c. 35 years old.
   d. 40 years old.

4. Because of high turnover in the House and in the Senate in the first half of the nineteenth century,
   a. seniority was very important.
   b. it was very difficult for junior members to become leaders in their parties.
   c. term limits were necessary.
   d. most of the action concerning public policy making occurred at the state level.

5. Power became decentralized from committee chairs to many members in the House in
   a. the 1860s.
   b. the 1890s.
   c. the 1920s.
   d. the 1970s.

6. What is the approximate reelection rate of incumbents in the House of Representatives?
   a. 50%
   b. 65%
   c. 90%
   d. 100%

7. The original gerrymander occurred in
   a. Massachusetts in 1812.
   b. Maine in 1876.
   c. Indiana in 1932.
   d. Kentucky in 1976.

8. Election results suggest that voters
   a. like their legislators in Congress.
   b. like the opponents to their legislators in Congress.
   c. believe that Congress is doing a good job.
   d. believe that Congress should be changed to a unicameral legislature.

9. Divided government
   a. was most prevalent in the early nineteenth century.
   b. has been common since the 1950s.
   c. ceased to be an issue with the election of President Ronald Reagan.
   d. None of the above.

10. Congress consists of _____ people.
    a. 100
    b. 293
    c. 435
    d. 535

11. Most of the work done in Congress is
    a. done in the committees.
    b. done on the floors of both the House and Senate.
    c. done by the party leaders.
    d. done in the conference committees.

12. Compared to their senate counterparts, House members
    a. serve on more committees.
    b. tend to be policy generalists.
    c. tend to be policy specialists.
    d. have a four-year term.

13. Most bills die
    a. at the subcommittee stage.
    b. on the floor of the House or Senate.
    c. when presidents exercise the veto power.
    d. when public opinion polls of the general public are taken.

14. Which of the following committees is charged with the task of resolving legislative differences between House and Senate versions of the same bill?
    a. Standing
    b. Select
    c. Special
    d. Conference

15. What was Strom Thurmond trying to defeat when he set the Senate filibuster record?
    a. A campaign finance reform bill.
    b. A civil rights bill.
    c. A defense appropriations bill.
    d. A welfare reform bill.

16. The Rules Committee
    a. regulates the conduct of House and Senate members when Congress is not in session.
    b. regulates how much money members can make outside their congressional salaries.
    c. regulates the flow of legislation in the Senate.
    d. regulates the flow of legislation in the House.

17. Members of Congress
    a. usually propose bills based on their own ideas.
    b. usually propose bills created by college professors.
    c. usually propose bills created by interest groups.
    d. usually propose bills created by many sources.

18. Which chamber is typically in session for many more days than its counterpart?
    a. The House of Representatives is typically in session longer than the Senate.
    b. The Senate is typically in session longer than the House of Representatives.
    c. Both chambers are in session the same amount of time.
    d. According to the Constitution, the Senate must stay in session 15 days longer than the House of Representatives every other year.

19. Congress typically passes _____ legislation.
    a. specific
    b. broad
    c. radical
    d. socialist

20. In the original Constitution, which of the following institutions was MOST democratic?
    a. Supreme Court
    b. Presidency
    c. House of Representatives
    d. Senate

Essays

21. Discuss the changes in the House of Representatives and the Senate since the early 1800s.
22. Discuss the nature of elections in the House and in the Senate. What kinds of advantages do incumbents enjoy as compared to challengers? Explain.
23. How does party leadership work in the House of Representatives and in the Senate? Be sure to include a discussion of both the majority and minority party leaders.
24. Discuss the legislative process in detail. Include all the stages of how a bill becomes a law.
25. What does representation of the people entail for members of Congress? Discuss the differing theories of representation. Which theory is most plausible in your opinion? Why?

CRITICAL THINKING EXERCISES

1. Write a letter to your U.S. representative and to both of your U.S. senators. Share your perspectives on an issue that is of importance to you, and solicit their perspectives on the same issue. Letters should be addressed in the following fashion:

    House of Representatives
    The Honorable _____
    United States House of Representatives
    Washington, D.C. 20515

    Senate
    The Honorable _____
    United States Senate
    Washington, D.C. 20510

2. Which individuals currently fill the following leadership positions in Congress? You can find out this information from a variety of sources (e.g., your instructor, reference librarian, *Congressional Quarterly Weekly Report*, calling your representative and/or senator).
    a.   Speaker of the House
    b.   House Majority Leader
    c.   House Majority Whip
    d.   House Minority Leader
    e.   House Minority Whip
    f.   Senate Majority Leader
    g.   Senate Majority Whip
    h.   Senate Minority Leader
    i.   Senate Minority Whip
    j.   President of the Senate
    k.   *President Pro Tempore* of the Senate

3. Using the *Congressional Quarterly Weekly Report* as your point of reference, find out the tenure for all the standing committee chairs in the House and in the Senate. Compute the average tenure for standing committee chairs in both chambers. How do the numbers compare? What do the figures illustrate about power in the U.S. Congress?

ANSWERS TO THE PRACTICE EXAM

1.	C	11.	A
2.	B	12.	C
3.	B	13.	A
4.	D	14.	D
5.	D	15.	B
6.	C	16.	D
7.	A	17.	D
8.	A	18.	B
9.	B	19.	B
10.	D	20.	C

21. Many changes have been witnessed in the House and in the Senate since the early 1800s. In the latter half of the nineteenth century in the House, civility replaced outrageous behavior because strict rules were developed to govern the conduct of members on the floor of the House and in committee meetings. A shift also occurred in the latter half of the nineteenth century. Members began to view their service as a career. Before, turnover was very high and more action existed at the state level. As a result of the high turnover, the Speaker exercised vast powers. As members began to serve longer, however, the Speaker lost a great deal of power. By the early part of this century, the seniority rule had evolved. Committee chairs were no longer appointed by the Speaker,

but based on the longest continuous service of a member of the majority party. From approximately 1910 to the 1970s, power in the House was concentrated in the hands of committee chairs and other senior members. This changed when a reform movement in the 1970s changed some rules taking power away from committee chairs and giving it to the chairs of subcommittees (the smaller units of a standing committee that oversee one component of the committee's jurisdiction). This change decentralized power in the House a great deal. The changes in the Senate have not been as dramatic as in the House. The Senate continues to operate under rules that reflect its small size. Senators continue to have the freedom of continuous debate, and individual senators can wield more influence over legislation than their counterparts in the House. In the mid-part of this century, senators had to endure lengthy apprenticeships before being able to exercise power. In the 1970s, the Senate adopted new rules that encouraged decentralization. As a result, power is more dispersed now than earlier. Junior senators no longer have to serve long apprenticeships before becoming power brokers.

22.   The nature of elections in the House and Senate contrast in two major ways. The difference in term lengths and, for most senators, differences in the number of people they represent influence the way representatives and senators get elected and how they behave in office. Yet one factor concerning congressional elections is quite striking. Incumbents in both the House and the Senate usually win (roughly 90% of the time in the House, and 80% of the time in the Senate). Incumbents in both chambers have many advantages in elections. These advantages include the opportunity to steer federal money into their districts and states, utilizing the resources of the office such as constituent service and the franking privilege, the ability to typically raise more campaign money than challengers, and the ultimate advantage of name recognition. In addition to these factors, the cost of trying to unseat an incumbent precludes many people from seeking election in the first place. Many are simply not willing to lose their current position to run in a risky election. In spite of these advantages, some challengers actually do unseat incumbents. Strong challengers usually have experience in politics, and they find it easier to raise campaign funds.

23.   Not unlike most organizations, Congress can only run effectively with leadership. Both the house and Senate have developed leadership structures to help them conduct their business. Each party organizes along slightly different lines. The House and Senate have similar leadership structures with the Speaker of the House being the only major difference between the two chambers. The Speaker is formally elected by the full House, but in reality is selected by members of the majority party before each two-year session. House rules afford the Speaker a great deal of authority. The Speaker is the chief parliamentary officer in the House, which enables this leader great control over the referral of legislation to committees, the scheduling of debates, and the recognition of members during the floor debate. The Speaker has considerable input on committee assignments. Informally, the Speaker can reward or punish members by granting, or withholding, favors. The Speaker can also control the flow of information in the House. Other important formal leaders are the majority leader and the majority whip. The majority leader also speaks for the majority party on the floor of the House. The majority whip is the chief vote counter for the Speaker. The whip informs members about the policy preferences of the House leadership. The minority party in the House is led by the minority leader and the minority whip. The minority leadership faces different types of problems than their counterparts. The opposition party will always lose unless it is unified and it attracts enough support from members of the majority party. Leadership in the Senate is both symbolic and substantive. It stipulates in the Constitution that the vice-president shall be president, or presiding officer, in the Senate. Usually the vice-president only appears in the Senate on ceremonial occasions, or in case of a tie vote. The Constitution further stipulates that in the absence of the vice-president, the *President Pro Tempore* shall preside over the Senate. Again, this is mostly an honorary position given to the senior majority party member. The substantive power rests with the majority and minority party leaders. The majority leader typically gets the most national media attention and becomes not only the spokesperson for the party, but a recognized political figure in national politics. Senate rules, however, do not afford the leaders to exercise as much power as their counterparts in the House. While the majority leader is in charge of the schedule, for example, even this power is limited by the other members. Most of the power is based on one's personal qualities, and not on formal structural rules.

24.   Lawmaking occurs in several stages. The process begins when a member of Congress formally introduces a bill. Only members can do this, although oftentimes the source of the legislation is not the representative or senator in question. Once a bill is introduced in the House or the Senate, it is referred to the appropriate committee. In the House, the Speaker decides what path the bill will take. In the Senate, the presiding officer decides. Both are largely constrained by the defined jurisdictions of the various committees. Usually, after the bill is sent to a standing committee, it is then referred to one of its subcommittees. Most bills die at this stage. If the subcommittee wants to proceed, it will hold hearings and usually mark-up the bill (go through it line by line). Once the bill passes the subcommittee, the entire process begins again in the full committee. More hearings and more mark-ups occur. If the bill passes in the full committee, it is sent to the floor of the House or Senate. In the House, the Rules Committee sets the conditions under which a bill will be considered by the full House. Most rules limit the amount of debate on the floor of the House. The number and types of amendments may also be limited. After debating and addressing amendments to the bill, a vote on the bill is taken. The Senate does not have an analogous Rules Committee. Bills are brought to the floor at the discretion of the majority leader. When a bill makes it to the floor of the Senate, debate is unlimited. After the debate is completed and any amendments are added, a vote is taken on the floor. Since we are assuming legislative success throughout, the House and Senate have passed different versions of the same bill. A conference committee consisting of senators and representatives is created to iron out the differences between the differing versions. All bills must be passed in identical language in both chambers in order to become law. Once this committee reaches an agreement, the bill is sent back to both chambers for another vote. If the House and Senate accept the compromise version, it is sent to the president. A president can sign the bill into law, veto it, do nothing and allow it to become law without his/her signature, or exercise a pocket veto.

25.   There are competing theories concerning representation of the people on the parts of members of Congress. One is the delegate theory of representation. This holds that members should vote according to the preferences of their constituents. Another is the trustee theory of representation, which maintains that voters have entrusted members with the responsibility of deciding what constitutes sound public policy. (Students should state which theory they find more plausible and why). Regardless of theoretical preferences, members of Congress are both free to vote as they desire and, at the same time, are constrained by constituent opinion. Ultimately, members of Congress must maintain the support of their constituents or they will not be returned to office.

SUMMARY

The Framers created the presidency in Article II of the Constitution. They did so because the experiment under the Articles of Confederation did not work. It became apparent that a national government could not function without a chief executive. In realizing this, however, the Framers were fearful of vesting too much power in any one person or one branch of government (the memory of King George III, in particular, was quite strong). As a result, the structural rules set forth in the Constitution try to balance the need for a strong executive with protections against the use of tyrannical power. Specific powers are delegated to the president, but many are shared with the other two branches of government.

OUTLINE

Opening Story: President Bill Clinton and the Christmas Tree Lighting Ceremony

In December of 1995, President Bill Clinton pressed the button on a switch first used by President Calvin Coolidge, thereby lighting the national Christmas tree. In his speech, he expressed his hopes for peace around the globe. The president's performance during the tree lighting ceremony illustrates the dual roles that are expected of American presidents. On one hand, President Clinton was fulfilling his ceremonial and nonpolitical duty as representative of the American people. At the same time, however, he was making political points as well. He was asking the public to understand and support the decision he made a month earlier to send U.S. troops to Bosnia. This merging of the nonpolitical and political roles is commonplace for presidents, as Americans expect them to be both a unifying symbol of the nation as well as a politically adept policy maker and leader.

The Development of the Presidency (p. 382)

The Presidency on Paper: Constitutional Rules (p. 382)

The Presidency in Practice: Applying the Rules (p. 386)

The Advent of the "Modern" Presidency (p. 388)

Selecting a President (p. 389)

The Nomination Process (p. 390)

The General Election (p. 396)

The Electoral College (p. 400)

Consequences for Governing (p. 402)

The Presidency as an Institution (p. 402)

The Powers of the Presidency (p. 402)

The Organizational Structure of the Presidency (p. 405)

The Workings of the Presidency (p. 409)

Assessing the Presidency as an Institution (p. 415)

The Presidency in American Politics (p. 415)

The Political Context: Permanent Crisis (p. 416)

Presidential Strategies (p. 418)

Presidential Relationships (p. 419)

Summary (p. 422)

Key Terms (p. 423)

Readings for Further Study (p. 424)

KEY TERMS, CONCEPTS, EVENTS, AND PEOPLE

Be able to identify and/or define each of the following and state its importance in a short paragraph.

Impeachment (p. 385)

Enumerated powers (p. 385)

Pocket veto (p. 386)

Implied powers (p. 386)

Caucus (p. 390)

Progressive movement (p. 391)

Frontloading (p. 395)

Independent expenditures (p. 398)

Soft money (p. 399)

Electoral college (p. 400)

Unit rule (p. 400)

Reprogramming authority (p. 403)

Central legislative clearance (p. 404)

Neutral competence (p. 413)

One Hundred Days (p. 417)

Midterm elections (p. 417)

Bargaining strategy (p. 418)

Going public strategy (p. 418)

Divided government (p. 420)

Executive order (p. 421)

LEARNING OBJECTIVES

After reading chapter 12, students should be able to:

1.   Identify the presidency's constitutionally defined features of institutional and political independence, possession of shared rather than unilateral powers, and ill-defined authority.
2.   Give examples from history of presidents who established precedents that their successors used to fulfill their duties.
3.   Explain why the presidency of Franklin Delano Roosevelt is said to mark the beginning of the "modern presidency."
4.   Describe the historical evolution of the presidential nomination process from congressional caucuses, through party conventions, to the present system.
5.   Identify and describe the main roles that modern presidents fulfill.

6.   Identify the three main stages by which the United States selects its presidents today.
7.   Identify the four changes in the presidential nomination process that resulted from the adoption of primary elections as the main method of choosing presidential candidates.
8.   Explain how the emergence of radio and television affected the conduct of presidential elections.
9.   Describe the key features of laws and Supreme Court decisions regarding presidential campaign financing, and identify the effects of those features on campaign spending by presidential candidates.
10. Explain the electoral college and discuss the effects the unit rule has on possible electoral outcomes.
11. Identify the three main sources of presidential power, and give an example of each type of source.
12. Compare and contrast the Restricted, Prerogative, and Stewardship Models of presidential authority.
13. Identify key differences in the institutional nature of the presidency before and after the creation of the Executive Office of the President in 1939.
14. Describe the functions of the presidential staff agencies in general, and of key agencies such as the White House Office, the Office of Management and Budget, the National Security Council, and the Office of the Vice President.
15. Compare and contrast the characteristics, advantages and disadvantages, and patterns in the use of the "pyramid" and "spokes-of-the-wheel" styles of presidential management.
16. Explain the difference between staff that are personally loyal to the president and those that adhere to the norm of neutral competence.
17. Explain the concept of institutionalization within the presidency and identify the consequences of its presence for the workings of the presidency.
18. Identify the features of the presidential context that make it a "permanent crisis."
19. Compare and contrast the "bargaining" and "going public" strategies that presidents use to exercise influence.
20. Characterize the nature of presidential leadership in the president's relationships with Congress, the bureaucracy, and the general public.

PRACTICE EXAM

(Answers appear at the end of this chapter)

Multiple Choice

1.   Presidents were limited to two full terms by
     a.   the Framers.
     b.   Article II of the Constitution.
     c.   a constitutional amendment.
     d.   Article I of the Constitution.

2.   Which president created a role for the president as a party leader?
     a.   George Washington
     b.   Thomas Jefferson
     c.   Andrew Jackson
     d.   Abraham Lincoln

3.   Which president established the era of the "modern presidency?"
     a.   Theodore Roosevelt
     b.   Woodrow Wilson
     c.   Franklin Delano Roosevelt
     d.   Ronald Reagan

4.   Who controlled the presidential nominating process from 1800-1824?
     a.   The general public.
     b.   King Caucus.
     c.   Party conventions.
     d.   The Progressives.

5.   The Progressives sought to
     a.   reform the political process AND reduce the influence of state party leaders.
     b.   eliminate the use of primary elections.
     c.   implement the spoils system.
     d.   do away with the New Hampshire Primary.

6.   Presidential candidates now spend over half of their campaign funds on
     a.   newspaper advertisements.
     b.   radio advertisements.
     c.   calling potential voters on the telephone.
     d.   television.

7. Independent expenditures have typically benefited _____ presidential candidates?
   a. Republican
   b. Democratic
   c. incumbent
   d. third party

8. How many total votes exist in the Electoral College?
   a. 270
   b. 435
   c. 535
   d. 538

9. What happens if no candidate receives a majority in the electoral college?
   a. The winner of the popular vote becomes president.
   b. The president is selected in the Senate.
   c. The president is selected in the House.
   d. The president is selected by the Supreme Court.

10. _____ helps the president draft the annual federal budget.
   a. The General Accounting Office
   b. The Congressional Budget Office
   c. The Office of Management and Budget
   d. The National Security Council

11. Presidential staff remained small and informal until
   a. 1789.
   b. 1829.
   c. 1877.
   d. 1939.

12. The National Security Council includes
   a. the president, vice president, secretary of state, and secretary of defense.
   b. the president, secretary of state, secretary of defense, and secretary of commerce.
   c. the president, attorney general, director of the Central Intelligence Agency, and director of the Office of Management and Budget.
   d. the president, vice president, secretary of treasury, and secretary of state.

13. The Office of the Vice President
   a. has remained the same since the time of John Adams.
   b. was powerful during the Progressive Era, but much less so today.
   c. has become less powerful since Walter Mondale was vice president from 1953-1957.
   d. has gained increased importance in recent years.

14. How did Ronald Reagan's management style compare to Bill Clinton's?
   a. President Reagan was more of a hands-on president than Bill Clinton.
   b. President Reagan utilized the spokes of the wheel style compared to President Clinton's pyramid style.
   c. President Reagan delegated a great deal of authority to his subordinates compared to President Clinton.
   d. Their management styles are very similar.

15. What did the Iran-Contra scandal illustrate?
   a. Presidents should delegate more authority to their subordinates.
   b. Presidents must be aware of the activities of their senior aides.
   c. Presidents are not bound by separation of powers if they do not wish to be.
   d. Richard Nixon would have been impeached by the House of Representatives had he not resigned.

16. Which of the following expectations has NOT been institutionalized by the presidency?
   a. Proposing legislation to the Congress.
   b. The State of the Union address before a joint session of Congress.
   c. Periodic press conferences.
   d. Giving presidential spouses a lot of influence in policy making.

17. In midterm elections,
   a. the president's party usually loses seats in Congress.
   b. the president's party usually gains seats in Congress.
   c. the president usually gets more support from the general public.
   d. None of the above.

18. What strategy did President Reagan utilize in 1981 to get congressional approval of tax and budget cuts?
    a. Going public strategy
    b. Bargaining strategy
    c. Arm twisting strategy
    d. Let's make a deal strategy

19. Who is the primary agenda setter in the U.S.?
    a. Congressional leaders
    b. Lobbyists
    c. Executive bureaucrats
    d. President

20. Since modern public opinion polling has been conducted, which president has achieved the highest approval rating?
    a. John Kennedy
    b. Ronald Reagan
    c. Dwight David Eisenhower
    d. George Bush

Essays

21. What are the enumerated powers of the president under Article II of the Constitution? Why is it that most of the authority of the presidency stems from implied powers? Explain.
22. What are the three different modes of nominating presidential candidates by political parties since the election of 1800? How do they differ?
23. Three conceptions of presidential power have evolved since George Washington's presidency. What are they and how do they differ? Be sure to give examples of each.
24. What ten agencies are included in the Executive Office of the President? What functions do they perform?
25. In order to achieve their goals and retain their stature as national leaders, presidents must maintain good relations with three important entities. What are they and how do Presidents cultivate positive relationships with them?

CRITICAL THINKING EXERCISES

1. Write a letter to president of the United States. Share your perspectives on an issue that is of importance to you, and solicit the president's view on the same issue. Letters should be addressed in the following fashion:

   The Honorable _____
   President of the United States
   The White House
   1600 Pennsylvania Avenue
   Washington, D.C. 20500

2. Write a brief critical analysis entitled, "The Best and the Worst U.S. Presidents." In it, identify the best and worst presidents in U.S. history. What criteria did you utilize to determine who was the best and who was the worst of all presidents? Be able to defend your selections.
3. Using Figure 12.5, develop a chronological list starting with the state with the highest number of electoral votes to the states with the lowest (do not forget the District of Columbia). At the very least, how many states must a candidate win to get a majority of the Electoral College (270 votes)? What does this tell you about the nature of presidential campaigns? Suppose you were either a member of Congress or a member of a state legislature and had to decide whether or not to support a constitutional proposal eliminating the Electoral College in favor of direct election of the president by the people. What would you decide? Why?

ANSWERS TO THE PRACTICE EXAM

1.	C	11.	D
2.	B	12.	A
3.	C	13.	D
4.	B	14.	C
5.	A	15.	B
6.	D	16.	D
7.	A	17.	A
8.	D	18.	A
9.	C	19.	D
10.	C	20.	D

21.　　Under Article II, the president is the commander in chief of the armed forces; the president has the power to pardon people for federal crimes; the president can make treaties with other countries (with Senate approval); the president has the power to appoint ambassadors and all federal judges including Supreme Court justices. The president must also inform Congress of the state of the union. Yet the brunt of presidential authority stems from the president's implied powers. Implied powers are powers that the presidency is assumed to have because they are necessary for executing the enumerated powers of the office. Many such powers are included in the constitutional clause stating that "the executive Power shall be vested in a President of the United States of America."

22.　　The three different modes of nominating presidential candidates by political parties include the congressional caucuses, party conventions, and direct primary elections. From 1800 to 1824, "King Caucus" selected presidential candidates. Both major political parties at the time developed this procedure. Members of Congress decided who would be nominated as president, and who would be reelected as well. After 1824, the caucus system began to break down. By 1832, the major parties established party conventions as the mode of nominating their presidential candidates. Local, county, and state conventions would take place, with state convention delegates choosing delegates to the national convention; the national delegates would chose the party's nominee. A third nomination mode began to evolve during the Progressive era, but took until 1972 to firmly take root. The advent of primary elections changed the rules of the presidential selection process. State party conventions no longer controlled the process; now the voters do so. The parties, as a result, have lost the power to control their own nominees to a large extent.

23.　　Past presidents have conformed to one of three conceptions of presidential power: the Restricted, Prerogative, and Stewardship Models. The most limited conception of presidential power is the Restricted Model. Adherents to this conception believe that presidents are permitted to exercise only those powers explicitly granted to them by the Constitution or statutory law. Presidents who adhere to this model tend to be very passive and reactive. An example is William Howard Taft. The most expansive conception of presidential power is the Prerogative Model, as was witnessed with the presidency of Abraham Lincoln. Under this conception of power, presidents may take any action to protect the integrity of the nation, whether it is legal or not. Lincoln violated the Constitution to achieve the higher goal of preserving the Union. Between both extremes is the Stewardship Model. Presidents under this conception have a duty to act as stewards of the national interest, as they alone represent the entire nation. In this role, presidents can take any action not explicitly prohibited by law or by the Constitution. Presidents following this model, such as Theodore Roosevelt, actively seek power and use it to lead the country. Most nineteenth century presidents adhered to the Restricted Model, whereas most modern presidents have conceived of their power in terms of the Stewardship Model.

24. Ten agencies are included in the Executive Office of the President. Each office provides advice and assistance to the president in differing policy matters:

1. Office of Management and Budget: helps the president formulate budget requests for government agencies and oversees management and implementation of government policies.

2. National Security Council: advises the president on foreign policy and national security issues. Provides analyses and advocacy of policy options.

3. National Economic Council: advises the president on economic policy issues.

4. Council of Economic Advisors: professional economists analyze economic conditions and trends in order to advise the president on economic policy.

5. White House Office: this includes the president's personal staff. The staff advises the president on policy, political, and electoral goals.

6. Domestic Policy Council: policy experts advise the president on a broad range of domestic policy issues.

7. Office of Science and Technology Policy: advises the president on scientific aspects of public policy.

8. Office of Administration: performs internal administrative duties such as personnel and budgeting for all agencies in the EOP.

9. Office of the Vice President: vice president's personal staff. Assists in fulfilling all duties assigned to the vice president by the president.

10. Office of the U.S. Trade Representative: studies and advises the president on foreign trade issues. Conducts trade negotiations for the government.

25. Presidents work with many groups both in and out of government to achieve their goals. It is imperative for presidents to maintain good relations with Congress, the bureaucracy, and the American public in particular. Presidents are expected to present a package of legislative proposals to Congress. Whether Congress enacts the proposals, however, depends partly on the relationship between the president and Congress. Presidents must also cultivate and nurture good relations within the federal bureaucracy so that bureaucrats will support and implement their programs. Although the president is supposedly the director of the federal bureaucracy, he or she cannot command the obedience of the various agencies. Presidents must instead bargain with agency members and attempt to persuade them to do his or her will. Finally, presidents must develop good relations with the general public. Presidents care a great deal about their approval ratings, as greater popularity usually means greater influence on Congress. As a result, presidents readily use their access to the media to try to shape the public's interpretation of significant events.

Chapter **13** The Federal Bureaucracy

SUMMARY

Under the Constitution, the power to oversee federal agencies belongs to both Congress and the president. The rules authorize Congress to create and fund agencies. On the other hand, presidents have the power to appoint senior agency officials so that their agencies faithfully enact the laws. As a result, the federal bureaucracy is not completely controlled by either. The rules that divide control of the bureaucracy between Congress and the presidency mean that federal agencies have some freedom to follow their own public policy objectives.

OUTLINE

Opening Story: Political Pressure and the Food and Drug Administration

In the mid-1980s, an alliance was forged between interest groups representing people with AIDS, members of Congress, and President Ronald Reagan. Since the 1960s, the Federal Drug Administration (FDA) has required pharmaceutical companies to demonstrate both the safety and effectiveness of new drugs before putting them on the market for consumers. Consequently, drug testing by the FDA had become an expensive process that usually took several years to complete. Groups representing AIDS patients criticized the FDA for taking too long to approve of new medicines for the deadly disease. President Reagan came to power with the general philosophy of reducing government regulation of the marketplace. As a result, the activists and the president forced the FDA to adopt new rules that eased access to experimental drugs for patients afflicted with life-threatening diseases. As a result, the length of time that the FDA takes to test drugs has plummeted. In 1987, the average new drug took three years to test. By 1992, this had decreased by almost one-half, to nineteen months. For drugs tested in a special drug approval program created in 1993, the rate was down to thirteen-and-a-half months.

What is Bureaucracy? (p. 427)

The Structure and Tasks of the Federal Bureaucracy (p. 428)

Types of Federal Agencies (p. 428)

The Tasks of the Federal Bureaucracy (p. 432)

Development of the Federal Bureaucracy (p. 434)

Constitutional Foundations (p. 434)

The Growth of the Federal Bureaucracy (p. 435)

The Expanding Functions of the Federal Bureaucracy (p. 436)

Changes in the Federal Bureaucracy's Personnel System (p. 439)

The Politics of the Federal Bureaucracy (p. 441)

The Political Character of the Federal Bureaucracy (p. 442)

The Goals of the Federal Bureaucracy (p. 445)

The Political Resources of the Federal Bureaucracy (p. 446)

Political Constraints on the Federal Bureaucracy (p. 449)

Iron Triangles and the Federal Bureaucracy (p. 454)

The Evolving Role of the Bureaucracy (p. 456)

Reinventing the Federal Bureaucracy (p. 457)

Summary (p. 459)

Key Terms (p. 460)

Readings for Further Study (p. 460)

KEY TERMS, CONCEPTS, EVENTS, AND PEOPLE

Be able to identify and/or define each of the following and state its importance in a short paragraph.

Bureaucracy (p. 426)

Bureaucrats (p. 427)

"Advice and consent" (p. 429)

Cabinet (p. 429)

Rule administration (p. 432)

Rule making (p. 432)

Rule adjudication (p. 433)

Spoils system (p. 439)

Patronage (p. 440)

Civil service (p. 440)

Clientele (p. 447)

Expertise (p. 448)

Iron triangles (p. 454)

Issue networks (p. 457)

LEARNING OBJECTIVES

After reading chapter 13, students should be able to:

1. Identify the five essential characteristics of bureaucracy.
2. Describe the differences among the four basic types of government agencies.
3. Define the bureaucratic tasks of rule administration, rule making, and rule adjudication.
4. Explain why the federal bureaucracy is a "constitutional hybrid."
5. Discuss how the size and missions of the federal bureaucracy have changed over the past two hundred years.
6. Describe how the federal government's personnel system has evolved over time.
7. Explain why bureaucracies are inherently political institutions.
8. Explain how administrative discretion, clientele support, and agency expertise serve as sources of political power for government agencies and discuss why some agencies are more powerful than others.
9. Describe the nature of the relationship between the federal bureaucracy and Congress.
10. Describe the nature of the relationship between the federal bureaucracy and the president.
11. Explain how interest groups try to influence how federal agencies operate.
12. Explain why and how agencies compete with one another for political power.
13. Describe the relationship between federal agencies and the courts.
14. Describe the three basic elements of an iron triangle and discuss how iron triangles affect government policy making.
15. Explain why so many attempts to make the federal bureaucracy more efficient and effective have failed.

PRACTICE EXAM

(Answers appear at the end of this chapter)

Multiple Choice

1. Who defined the ideal bureaucracy?
   a. Max Weber
   b. James Watt
   c. Woodrow Wilson
   d. Norton Long

2. Every type of government agency administers
   a. the president's policy objectives.
   b. Congress' policy objectives.
   c. rules.
   d. the will of the majority.

3. Which of the following is an example of an independent agency?
   a. Tennessee Valley Authority
   b. Federal Communications Commission
   c. Department of Agriculture
   d. National Aeronautics and Space Administration

4. The most basic function of any agency is
   a. rule adjudication.
   b. rule administration.
   c. rule making.
   d. rule violation.

5. The federal government currently employs about
   a. 500,000 civilians.
   b. 1,000,000 civilians.
   c. 3,000,000 civilians.
   d. 10,000,000 people.

6. The first Congress created
   a. the Departments of State, War, Treasury, and the Attorney General.
   b. the Departments of State, Interior, Treasury, and the Postmaster General.
   c. the Departments of State, Education, Treasury, and the Solicitor General.
   d. the Departments of State, War, Agriculture, and Labor.

7. The number of federal civilian employees per capita has _____ since 1951.
   a. increased dramatically
   b. increased slightly
   c. stayed about the same
   d. decreased

8. Who benefits from income redistribution?
   a. Poor people.
   b. Rich people.
   c. Poor people and rich people.
   d. Corporate farmers.

9. What event prompted the passage of the Pendleton Act?
   a. The Civil War.
   b. The Great Depression.
   c. World War II.
   d. The assassination of James Garfield.

10. Federal agencies are
    a. political institutions.
    b. neutral institutions.
    c. Democratic institutions.
    d. Republican institutions.

11. James Watt and Bruce Babbitt have both served
    a. in Congress.
    b. as Secretary of Commerce.
    c. as Secretary of Interior.
    d. as Chair of the Federal Election Commission.

12. When one federal agency grows in size and power,
    a. other agencies do the same.
    b. interest group lobbying ends.
    c. it almost always makes enemies.
    d. None of the above.

13. Bureaucratic imperialism refers to
    a. red tape.
    b. competition to become the lead organization in a given policy area.
    c. the explosion in the size of the federal bureaucracy.
    d. the tendency of all bureaucracies to be slow.

14. Which of the following is NOT a part of the iron triangle alliance?
    a. Supreme Court
    b. Congressional committee or subcommittee
    c. Political interest group
    d. Government agency

15. Iron triangles are most effective
    a. when they form around broad policy issues.
    b. when they form around narrow policy issues.
    c. when they form around philosophical issues.
    d. when they form around liberal issues.

16. Agencies can use their _____ to ensure that their policy preferences are followed.
    a. mission goals
    b. survival goals
    c. legal constraints
    d. expertise

17. The Cuban Missile Crisis demonstrated that
    a. agencies always cooperate in a crisis.
    b. agencies sometimes fight among themselves.
    c. bureaucratic squabbling is limited to foreign policy matters.
    d. None of the above.

18. Iron triangles
    a. are more powerful than ever.
    b. have disappeared in American politics.
    c. are less of a force in American politics ever since World War I.
    d. are less of a force in American politics ever since the 1970s.

19. Plans to make the bureaucracy more efficient
    a. date back to President Theodore Roosevelt.
    b. rarely draw bipartisan support.
    c. have been successful over the last three decades.
    d. date back to President Ronald Reagan.

20. The decision to rewrite the rules to deregulate the savings and loan industry
    a. made banks more efficient.
    b. did not result in much change for the general public.
    c. will cost American taxpayers billions of dollars.
    d. helped to reduce the national deficit.

Essays

21.   According to Max Weber, what is the ideal type of bureaucracy? What characteristics are typical of the ideal bureaucracy? Do American bureaucracies today exhibit these characteristics?

22.   What are the four main kinds of organizations within the federal bureaucracy? How are they different? Be sure to give examples of each.

23.   Describe the changes that have occurred in the bureaucracy's personnel system since the beginning of the republic.

24.   Why do agencies want to exercise political power? How do they develop power?

25.   In the 1992 presidential election, Bill Clinton pledged to "reinvent government" to make it more efficient and effective. A year later, a task force led by Vice President Al Gore produced a report called *From Red Tape to Results: Creating a Government That Works Better and Costs Less.* Why do most presidents meet with little success in attempting to reform the federal bureaucracy?

CRITICAL THINKING EXERCISES

1.   Quiz your knowledge of the current cabinet secretaries. How many can you name correctly? (Your instructor or a reference librarian can readily assist you with obtaining a correct list, if required).

        Secretary of State:
        Secretary of Treasury:
        Secretary of Defense:
        U.S. Attorney General:
        Secretary of Interior:
        Secretary of Agriculture:
        Secretary of Commerce:
        Secretary of Labor:
        Secretary of Health and Human Services:
        Secretary of Housing and Urban Development:
        Secretary of Transportation:
        Secretary of Energy:
        Secretary of Education:
        Secretary of Veterans Affairs:

2.   Write an analysis entitled "The Inner and Outer Cabinet." In your essay, explain which executive departments typically have a great deal of influence on the president (and therefore are part of the inner cabinet) and which departments typically do not render a great deal of influence on the president (and therefore are part of the outer cabinet). Most importantly, why is this the case? How do you account for exceptions to the rule? Explain.

3.   Some analysts are debating the feasibility of elevating the Environmental Protection Agency (EPA) from an independent agency to an executive department. This would make the EPA the fifteenth executive department in the bureaucracy. Is this a good idea or not? Why? (Base your response on your philosophy of government, your political beliefs, and your policy perspectives concerning the environment).

ANSWERS TO THE PRACTICE EXAM

1.	A	11.	C
2.	C	12.	C
3.	D	13.	B
4.	B	14.	A
5.	C	15.	B
6.	A	16.	D
7.	D	17.	B
8.	C	18.	D
9.	D	19.	A
10.	A	20.	C

21. Weber's ideal type of bureaucracy has five characteristics: specialization, hierarchy, formality, record-keeping, and professionalization. Specialization entails a well-defined division of labor in which jobs are divided and assigned to subgroups within the organization that have special expertise with specific tasks. Hierarchy is a clear chain of command in which workers are arranged in order of their rank or authority. Formality occurs when organizations establish a set of rules and procedures that are designed to ensure that it performs its duties in a consistent fashion. Record-keeping involves retaining documented records of organizational decisions and activities. Professionalization exists when organizations are staffed with full-time, career workers who are paid a regular salary and who are hired and promoted on the basis of their competence in carrying out assigned duties. Bureaucracies in the United States today generally exhibit most of the Weberian characteristics. Most of the agencies at the federal level are permanent organizations in which workers are assigned to different levels on the basis of their authority. Most also follow a set of rules in carrying out their specialized tasks that transcend time, and all agencies are required by law to keep records. In terms of organizational staffing, most employees in the federal bureaucracy hold permanent positions and are career-oriented. At least in principle, the vast majority of people are hired and promoted on the basis of merit.

22. The four main kinds of organizations within the federal bureaucracy are executive departments, independent regulatory commissions, government corporations, and independent agencies. Executive departments (e.g., State, Treasury, and Defense) are the primary form of organization in the bureaucracy. There are fourteen in all. They are headed by a single individual (usually called the secretary). These fourteen secretaries make up the president's cabinet, a group designed to advise the president on policy matters. Executive departments are typically quite large, but in practice most presidents make little use of the cabinet and instead rely on the White House staff. All independent regulatory commissions (e.g., Federal Communications Commission, Federal Reserve Board, and the Nuclear Regulatory Commission) perform the same basic function: they try to promote the public interest by writing and enforcing rules that regulate the operations of private industry. Most are much smaller than executive departments. Instead of being headed by a single individual, most are headed by a commission. Independent regulatory commissions have greater political independence from the president than do executive departments. This is due to the fact that commissioners are appointed for fixed terms that are staggered over time. A third type of bureaucratic organization is the government corporation (e.g., Federal Deposit Insurance Corporation, Tennessee Valley Authority, and Federal Financing Bank). These are government-owned companies that sell services or products to the public and thereby generate their revenues. Some are headed by single individuals, and some by several persons. In principle they are self-supporting agencies in that they sell their services at prices so that they can break even each year. When they fail to do so, however, the federal government supplements the corporation's income. The final category of independent agencies (e.g., Environmental Protection Agency, National Aeronautics and Space Administration, and the Peace Corps) includes all other types of federal agencies. They are not part of any executive department, and their leaders do not have the cabinet-level status of departments. Some are headed by individuals, and some by commission. Typically, independent agencies do not have the same prestige as that of executive departments.

23. Dramatic changes have occurred in the bureaucracy's personnel system over the last 200 years. From 1789 to 1829, the federal bureaucracy recruited its workers primarily from the elite classes in American society. Service in the bureaucracy was viewed as a high calling, and was typically limited to those who were loyal to the political party in power, who had high social standing, and who had relatives in government. This era, called government by gentleman, gave way to the spoils system with the inauguration of Andrew Jackson as president in 1829. Under the spoils system, the practice of hiring and firing bureaucrats was based on party loyalty and support in election campaigns. Government jobs as a result went to the victor in an election. Presidents could reward their loyal supporters with government jobs. This political patronage was helpful to presidents in building support for their proposals. The spoils system lasted into the 1880s. A drawback to the spoils system is that it bred public cynicism about the integrity of federal employees. This was a time when political corruption was quite high. A reform movement to change the system so that government service would be based upon competence rather than political considerations gained momentum in 1881 with the assassination of President James Garfield by a disappointed office seeker. The Pendleton Act, passed by Congress in 1883, established the third new system: civil service (also called the merit system). In this new system, hiring, promotion, and firing decisions are based on individual merit, and not on patronage. Originally, this only effected about 10% of the federal bureaucracy. Today, over 80% of all bureaucrats fall under some category of the civil service system.

24. Agencies want to exercise political power because their views on what constitutes judicious public policy may differ greatly than those held by the general public, members of Congress, and other government agencies. They also want to ensure their own survival. Agencies which are successful at building their own power bases can protect their interests against rivals and even expand their influence over public policy. The building of power bases generally occurs through administrative discretion, clientele support, and agency expertise. Agencies can develop power through rule-making. Since they exercise discretion in deciding how to administer policy, they can use it to implement policies that reflect their views on what constitutes good public policy. In addition to the power that comes from discretion in the implementation of policy, the two main sources of power for a government agency are the support of its clientele and its expertise. Because agencies differ on both counts, they also differ in the amount of political power they muster. An agency's clientele includes those groups that receive the services provided by agency programs (usually special interest groups). Powerful agencies have powerful clientele groups. Agencies that are supported by large, well-organized, and well-funded groups are far more likely to achieve their objectives than agencies which lack such support. Agencies also can gain political power from the expertise of their employees. Many civil servants acquire a great deal of technical expertise about their policy areas. As a result, members of Congress and the president are often inclined to accept the agency's policy proposals, as they do not have the same comparative specialized knowledge.

25. Efforts to make the federal bureaucracy more effective and efficient generally draw bipartisan support. Yet many presidents in the twentieth century, beginning with President Theodore Roosevelt, have attempted to do just this but have achieved little success. Many recommendations to rewrite bureaucratic rules are proposed and then abandoned. The political costs are generally too high. When it comes to reducing agency budgets, the president must receive congressional approval. Defenders of the agencies and programs targeted for major changes will lobby their allies in Congress intensively. As a result, most presidents abandon their reform efforts because they determine that fighting Congress and agencies will not result in very many political benefits.

SUMMARY

The federal judiciary was created by Article III of the Constitution. Only the Supreme Court was specifically created by the Constitution; the Framers delegated the task of designing a court system to Congress. They envisioned that federal judges and Supreme Court justices would only interpret the laws and policies passed by Congress and the president. Early on in the public's history, however, the federal courts became policy-making institutions in their own right. The doctrine of judicial review became a part of American jurisprudence in *Marbury v. Madison* (1803). This does not mean, however, that the policy-making power of the courts is equivalent to that of the president and Congress. The power of the federal courts is limited in a number of ways, including the reactive nature of courts, the inability of courts to enforce their decisions, the ability of the president and Congress to draft new laws, and the impact of public opinion.

OUTLINE

Opening Story: Free speech and the Supreme Court Justices

In 1995, a unanimous Supreme Court ruled in *Rubin v. Coors Brewing Co.* that a federal law preventing brewers from listing a beer's alcohol content on the label violated their right to free speech under the First Amendment. The law had been written just after the end of Prohibition, and it reflected the federal government's desire to prevent brewers from luring customers on the basis of higher alcohol content. The Supreme Court sided with Coors Brewing Company, which opposed the law. The justices deemed that the regulation was irrational and invalidated it. Now Americans can learn how much alcohol is in their beer by simply looking at the label. The Supreme Court's ruling in *Rubin* illustrates that every day judges make decisions that affect the way Americans live. Yet Americans have no direct input in who sits on the Supreme Court or any other federal court, and in a number of states they have only a limited say over who serves on state courts. In spite of the undemocratic nature of the Supreme Court, an independent judiciary is crucial in all democracies, for it protects the rights of the individuals and restrains the government from abusing its authority.

The Federal Courts (p. 462)

The Constitution and the Federal Courts (p. 462)

Congress and the Federal Courts (p. 463)

The Federal Court System (p. 464)

The Federal Courts as Policy Makers (p. 466)

Judicial Review, Judicial Activism, and Policy Making (p. 466)

Limitations on the Courts (p. 468)

The Supreme Court as a Political Institution (p. 469)

The Characteristics of the Court (p. 470)

The Politics of Nomination and Confirmation (p. 473)

Presidential Legacies on the Supreme Court (p. 475)

Decision Making at the Supreme Court (p. 475)

Hearing a Case (p. 475)

Individual Decision Making (p. 477)

Supreme Court Opinions (p. 480)

Voting Patterns (p. 481)

Who Wins Before the Supreme Court? (p. 482)

The Lower Federal Courts (p. 483)

District Courts (p. 483)

Courts of Appeal (p. 483)

Nomination and Confirmation (p. 483)

State Courts (p. 485)

Organization (p. 485)

Judicial Selection (p. 485)

Length of Service (p. 486)

State Laws (p. 486)

Summary (p. 487)

Key Terms (p. 488)

Readings for Further Study (p. 489)

KEY TERMS, CONCEPTS, EVENTS, AND PEOPLE

Be able to identify and/or define each of the following and state its importance in a short paragraph.

Constitutional courts (p. 464)

Legislative courts (p. 464)

110

Marbury v. Madison (p. 466)

Judicial review (p. 467)

Judicial activism (p. 467)

Writ of certiorari (p. 475)

Rule of Four (p. 476)

Amicus curiae (p. 476)

Stare decisis (p. 477)

Majority opinion (p. 480)

Concurring opinion (p. 481)

Dissenting opinion (p. 481)

Senatorial courtesy (p. 483)

Missouri Plan/Merit System (p. 486)

LEARNING OBJECTIVES

After reading chapter 14, students should be able to:

1. Describe the system of federal courts and distinguish between constitutional and legislative courts.
2. Identify what the Constitution says about the structure and powers of the federal court system and describe the development of the courts' policy-making powers—including *Marbury v. Madison* and the doctrine of judicial review.
3. Distinguish between judicial review and judicial activism and identify the contending arguments in the debate over how far the courts should go in making public policy.
4. Discuss the limitations on the power of the courts: their reactive nature, their inability to enforce their rulings, the ability of the president and Congress to write new laws, and the force of public opinion.
5. Identify what sorts of people serve on the Supreme Court and how they get there.
6. Explain the politics of the nomination and confirmation process and discuss why Supreme Court justices are sometimes described as a president's legacy.
7. Describe the process and the politics leading to the Supreme Court's decision to hear a case.
8. Explain the roles of individual beliefs and precedent in justices' decisions—including the role of *stare decisis*.
9. Explain how the Supreme Court makes decisions and communicates them to the public, including the roles of majority, concurring, and dissenting opinions.
10. Describe voting patterns on the Supreme Court in recent years.
11. Explain how lower court judges are selected, including the role of senatorial courtesy.
12. Describe the various state court systems, including how judges are selected.
13. Recognize the wide range of variation in laws from state to state.

PRACTICE EXAM

(Answers appear at the end of this chapter)

Multiple Choice

1. The federal court system was created
   a. by the Constitution.
   b. by Congress.
   c. by the president.
   d. by the Constitution and by Congress.

2. Which of the following has the constitutional power to create new federal courts?
   a. Supreme Court
   b. President
   c. Congress
   d. Executive bureaucracy

3. Which president attempted to "pack the Court?"
   a. George Washington
   b. Thomas Jefferson
   c. Ulysses S. Grant
   d. Franklin Delano Roosevelt

4. The Supreme Court has consisted of nine justices since
   a. 1789.
   b. 1803.
   c. 1869.
   d. 1911.

5. At the present time, there are _____ courts of appeal and _____ district courts at the federal level.
   a. 7, 256
   b. 13, 94
   c. 21, 178
   d. 45, 512

6. The doctrine of judicial review was established by the Supreme Court in
   a. 1803.
   b. 1857.
   c. 1896.
   d. 1937.

7. The Supreme Court outlawed segregated schools in
   a. *Plessy v. Ferguson.*
   b. *Brown v. Board of Education.*
   c. *Swann v. Charlotte-Mecklenberg Board of Education.*
   d. *Milliken v. Bradley.*

8. Who is currently the Chief Justice of the United States?
   a. Warren Burger
   b. William Rehnquist
   c. Earl Warren
   d. Sandra Day O'Connor

9. Which of the following is an example where an attempt to overturn a Supreme Court decision was *not successful*?
   a. lowering the voting age to 18
   b. State restrictions on religious practices
   c. Flag burning
   d.. Cutting the federal deficit

10. Which of the following statements is *true?*
    a. Five women have served on the U.S. Supreme Court.
    b. Twelve African Americans have served on the U.S. Supreme Court.
    c. No Jewish Americans have ever served on the U.S. Supreme Court.
    d. No Asian Americans, Native Americans, or Hispanic Americans have ever served on the U.S. Supreme Court.

11. Which of the following Supreme Court nominations was rejected by the U.S. Senate?
    a. Douglas Ginsburg
    b. Lewis Powell
    c. Robert Bork
    d. Clarence Thomas

12. Most cases arrive to the Supreme Court by
    a. a writ of certification.
    b. original jurisdiction.
    c. a writ of *certiorari.*
    d. a writ of errors.

13. How long does oral argument last for each Supreme Court case?
    a. The defendant and the plaintiff can take as long as they desire.
    b. The defendant and the plaintiff each have 30 minutes.
    c. The defendant and the plaintiff each have 4 hours.
    d. The defendant and the plaintiff each have 8 hours.

14. What important judicial principle was exercised in *Planned Parenthood of Southeastern Pennsylvania v. Casey* (1992)?
    a. *Stare decisis*
    b. *Amicus curiae*
    c. Judicial activism
    d. Judicial self-restraint

15. When does a decision become final in the Supreme Court?
    a. When 3 justices agree on an issue.
    b. When 5 or more justices agree on an issue.
    c. When all 9 justices agree on an issue.
    d. When the rule of 4 is invoked.

16. If the Chief Justice sides with the minority, who assigns the task of writing the majority opinion?
    a. The Chief Justice still assigns the duty.
    b. The oldest justice in the majority decides who will write it.
    c. The justices in the majority take a vote.
    d. The most senior justice in the majority assigns the task.

17. Which chief justice served from 1953-1969, and was known for liberal decisions?
    a. Chief Justice Harlan Stone
    b. Chief Justice Warren Burger
    c. Chief Justice Earl Warren
    d. Chief Justice William Rehnquist

18. Most federal cases are
    a. criminal cases.
    b. civil cases.
    c. tax cases.
    d. administrative cases.

19. Which of the following appointed the most minorities to the federal bench?
    a. Gerald Ford
    b. Jimmy Carter
    c. Ronald Reagan
    d. George Bush

20. While federal district courts handle approximately 280,000 cases each year, approximately how many cases are handled by state courts?
    a. 500,000
    b. 1,000,000
    c. 20,000,000
    d. 100,000,000

Essays

21.   Explain how federal and state cases can end up in the U.S. Supreme Court.
22.   Alexander Hamilton argued that by its very nature, the judiciary would always be the weakest branch of government. Has history proved him right? What major factors curb the power of the courts?
23.   Explain how presidential nominations to the Supreme Court can become contentious in the U..S. Senate. Be sure to cite examples in your response.
24.   Explain the role of precedent in *Planned Parenthood of Southeastern Pennsylvania v. Casey* (1992).
25.   How does partisan politics influence the appointment of federal judges to the courts of appeals and to the district courts?

CRITICAL THINKING EXERCISES

1. Obtain the following information:
    a. Who are the nine justices currently serving on the U.S. Supreme Court?
    b. When were they confirmed by the U.S. Senate?
    c. Which president appointed them?
    d. How old are the justices?
    e. What was their political party affiliation at the time of their appointment to the Court?
        After reviewing this information, write an essay entitled "The Judicial Philosophy of Today's Supreme Court." (You may wish to review pp. 466-468 in the text).
2. Obtain a copy of Chief Justice John Marshall's opinion in *Marbury v. Madison*, 1 Cranch 137 (1803). Reflecting on the Chief Justice's reasoning, write an essay entitled "John Marshall, the Constitution, and the Doctrine of Judicial Review."
3. Under the Constitution, all federal judges are appointed for life and "hold their Offices during good Behaviour." Most states do not follow the federal model for judicial selection, and most state judges serve for specific terms. Find out the mode(s) of judicial selection in your state and compare it to the federal level. Also determine how long judges may serve at the different levels within the court structure in your state. Which system is more optimum? Why?

ANSWERS TO THE PRACTICE EXAM

1.	D	11.	C
2.	C	12.	C
3.	D	13.	B
4.	C	14.	A
5.	B	15.	B
6.	A	16.	D
7.	B	17.	C
8.	B	18.	B
9.	C	19.	B
10.	D	20.	D

21. In the federal court system, the district courts are almost always the courts of original jurisdiction. These courts are presided by single judges who determine guilt or innocence in federal criminal trials, or assess fault in federal civil cases. About 10% of these cases are appealed to the next level, the federal courts of appeals. The circuit courts of appeals comprise the middle tier of the federal system. These appellate courts hear appeals of decisions made by the district courts and some administrative agencies. The Supreme Court justices may decide to review a case decided in one of the courts of appeals, although this occurs only a small percentage of the time. Cases can also arrive to the Supreme Court by other means—most notably when a state's highest court renders a decision based on an important federal issue. The most common path, however, is within the federal system beginning at the district court stage and then moving on to the courts of appeals.

22. Despite some significant cases where the justices made public policy (e.g., *Brown v. Board of Education*, *Roe v. Wade*), Hamilton's prophesy has remained true in U.S. history. Four major factors curb the power of courts: the reactive nature of courts, the inability to enforce their rulings, the ability of the president and Congress to draft new laws, and public opinion. Courts are reactive by their very nature—judges cannot seek out cases to decide. If the Supreme Court justices, for example, want to change a policy, they have to wait to have a case before them that deals with the specific issue they want to address. Congress and the president can initiate policy making at any time. The courts must also depend on other government agencies to enforce their decisions. Even though *Brown v. Board of Education* was decided over forty years ago, school desegregation has not been fully implemented in the U.S. Furthermore, the power of the courts is limited by the ability of

Congress and the president to write new laws. Congress, for example, can react to a Supreme Court decision by initiating a proposal to amend the Constitution. Lastly, judges are constrained by public opinion. Many believe that the Supreme Court's authority rests with the confidence of the general public. The political process by which judges are appointed has helped to insure that judges are in touch with mainstream public opinion.

23. Presidential nominations to the U.S. Supreme Court can become contentious for many reasons. If the president is perceived as weak politically, the Senate becomes more willing to challenge the nomination. In 1968, for example, President Lyndon Johnson announced that he would not seek another term in office. When he tried to fill a Court vacancy, the Republicans succeeded in blocking it until President Nixon took office. A president's nominees may also run into trouble if his or her party is in the minority in the Senate. This occurred in 1969, 1970, and 1987 when the Senate which was controlled by Democrats in all three years rejected the nominations of Clement Haynsworth, Harrold Carswell, and Robert Bork, respectively. All three were appointed by Republican presidents (Nixon and Reagan). Nominations can also become embroiled in controversy if the nominees are perceived to lack the proper credentials fitting for a Supreme Court justice, or if they have exhibited improper behavior. Harrold Carswell's credentials were deemed very weak when Nixon appointed him to the Court. Another nominee, Douglas Ginsburg, had to withdraw his nomination when it became known that he used marijuana while he was a law professor. President Bush's nomination of Clarence Thomas was almost defeated when allegations of sexual harassment against him became public. Finally, a nomination to the Supreme Court can become contentious if a nominee's legal and political views clash with those of powerful senators. Such was the case with Robert Bork. His legal views were challenged by liberal senators who felt that his positions on a wide variety of legal and social issues were too conservative.

24. At issue in *Planned Parenthood of Southeastern Pennsylvania v. Casey* was the constitutionality of a Pennsylvania law that imposed restrictions on abortion. The law did not ban abortions, but pro-choice advocates wanted the Court to strike down Pennsylvania's law as unconstitutional. Abortion opponents hoped that the Court would use this case to overturn *Roe v. Wade* (1973), the case that legalized abortions in the first place. The role of precedent, or *stare decisis*, was very significant in this case. A majority of the justices decided against overturning *Roe* on the basis that changing the precedent would cause profound damage to the integrity and legitimacy of the Court. The dissenters believed that *Roe* was wrongly decided, and as such it was the Court's responsibility to overturn its earlier precedent.

25. Partisan politics clearly influences the appointment of federal judges. Like Supreme Court justices, district and appeals court judges are nominated by the president and confirmed by the U.S. Senate. Unlike the selection for Supreme Court justices, however, members of the Senate have a great deal of input in the selection of federal judges. Most of the time, presidents adhere to a tradition called senatorial courtesy. This occurs when a president asks a senior senator in his or her party from the state or region where a vacancy exists to supply a list of possible nominees. If there is no senator in the state or region, a president can obtain a list from a member of the House of Representatives or a state party leader. Presidents generally refrain from nominating a candidate who does not enjoy the support of party members in the given state or region.

Chapter 15 The Federal System and State Government

SUMMARY

Prior to the New Deal programs implemented in the 1930s, the federal government did not work closely with state and local governments. During the presidency of Franklin D. Roosevelt, however, the increase in federal assistance to the subordinate levels of government increased dramatically. As a result, the era of dual federalism ended, and the New Deal ushered in the era of fiscal federalism where the federal government has played a major role in financing the programs and policies of state and local governments.

OUTLINE

Opening Story: The National Highway System Bill of 1995

The Republican congressional leaders of the 104th Congress pledged to shift many powers from the federal government back to the states. In keeping with this pledge, Congress passed the National Highway System bill, which allowed states to set their own speed limits on the nation's highways and to decide whether to require motorcyclists to wear helmets. But while Congress did return control of many transportation and safety matters to the states, it retained federal power in other areas. Congress, for example, maintained seat belt requirements. It even imposed a new demand on the states, requiring them to adopt "zero tolerance" laws that would make it illegal for underage drinkers to drive or risk losing some federal highway funds.

      This case study demonstrates a couple of points about American politics. First, the rules governing the relationship between the federal and state governments are important, because they determine how much influence the federal government wields over the states. Secondly, the rules within the states are also important, for they determine the policies that affect the everyday lives of citizens. In the American federal system of government, a combination of rules at the federal and state levels determine the policies that govern peoples' lives.

Relations Between Federal, State, and Local Government (p. 494)

Federal Aid to State and Local Governments (p. 494)

Other Forms of Federal Influence (p. 499)

The Changing Nature of Federalism (p. 500)

State Government and Politics (p. 502)

State Constitutions (p. 503)

Governors (p. 503)

State Legislatures (p. 507)

Interest Groups in State Politics (p. 511)

The Public and Direct Democracy (p. 514)

Summing Up (p. 516)

State Budgets (p. 517)

Raising Revenues (p. 517)

Budgeting (p. 520)

Spending (p. 521)

Local Government (p. 521)

Forms of Local Government (p. 521)

Local Government Structures (p. 522)

Local Government and Representation (p. 522)

The Costs of Local Government (p. 523)

Privatization of Government Services (p. 523)

Who Delivers?: Public Opinion and Level of Government (p. 524)

Summary (p. 525)

Key Terms (p. 526)

Readings for Further Study (p. 526)

KEY TERMS, CONCEPTS, EVENTS, AND PEOPLE

Be able to identify and/or define each of the following and state its importance in a short paragraph.

Dual federalism (p. 495)

Fiscal federalism (p. 495)

Categorical grants-in-aid (p. 496)

Block grants (p. 496)

General revenue sharing (p. 496)

Mandates (p. 499)

"Picket-fence" federalism (p. 500)

Lame duck (p. 503)

Line-item veto (p. 505)

Executive amendment (p. 505)

Direct democracy (p. 514)

Referendum (p. 514)

Initiative (p. 514)

"Rainy day" fund (p. 520)

Privatization (p. 523)

LEARNING OBJECTIVES

After reading chapter 15, students should be able to:

1. Describe the changing relations between federal, state, and local governments—including the ideas of dual federalism and fiscal federalism.
2. Identify the different forms of financial aid to cities and states, including categorical grants-in-aid, block grants, and general revenue sharing.
3. Define and explain the importance of mandates and picket-fence federalism.
4. Recognize that most state governments generally mirror the federal government in their organization.
5. Recognize that most state constitutions are longer than the U.S. Constitution and explain why state constitutions generally are amended much more frequently than is the U.S. Constitution.
6. Explain the central role of governors in state government, discuss what sorts of people become governors, and discuss the formal and informal powers that governors have in most states—including powers such as the line-item veto and the executive amendment.
7. Discuss the diversity of state legislatures in terms of size, professionalization, and membership.
8. Discuss elections for state legislatures, including their turnover rates and the effects of term limits.
9. Describe the role interest groups play in state government and identify the sorts of regulations that states have adopted to limit their influence.
10. Identify the tools of direct democracy—including the varieties of referenda, initiatives, and recall votes—and recognize the power these tools give to the public.
11. Explain how states craft their budgets, including the range of methods they use to generate revenues and the sorts of programs on which they spend their money.
12. Discuss the differences between the federal government and state government when it comes to budgeting—including the line-item veto and balanced-budget requirements of some states.
13. Identify the variety of levels and organizational styles of local government—including the mayor-council, city-commission, and council-manager styles of city government.
14. Recognize the growing number of relationships between local governments and the federal government.

PRACTICE EXAM

(Answers appear at the end of this chapter)

Multiple Choice

1. During the 1800s, what was the most common form of federal aid to the states?
   a. Block grants
   b. Categorical grants
   c. Land
   d. Revenue sharing

2. When did the tradition of dual federalism collapse?
   a. Civil War
   b. World War I
   c. New Deal
   d. World War II

3. During Ronald Reagan's presidency, the federal government's contribution to state and local revenues
   a. increased dramatically.
   b. increased by a small percentage.
   c. stayed about the same as when Jimmy Carter was president.
   d. decreased.

4. Categorical grants-in-aid were particularly popular in
   a. the 1860s.
   b. the 1960s.
   c. the 1970s.
   d. the 1980s.

5. What is the oldest operative constitution in the U.S.?
   a. The Massachusetts Constitution.
   b. The U.S. Constitution.
   c. The Alabama Constitution.
   d. The Hawaii Constitution.

6. Which of the following is NOT true?
   a. State constitutions are typically much longer than the U.S. Constitution.
   b. State constitutions are more stable than the U.S. Constitution.
   c. State constitutions are easier to amend than the U.S. Constitution.
   d. Most states have had several constitutions.

7. Approximately what percentage of citizens can typically identify the name of their state governor?
   a. 90%
   b. 75%
   c. 50%
   d. 35%

8. Most state governors in the U.S. have a _____ year term.
   a. 2
   b. 3
   c. 4
   d. 6

9. 43 states give their governors the
   a. line-item veto.
   b. power to reduce spending provisions in legislative bills.
   c. executive amendment.
   d. Vanna White amendment.

10. The only state with a unicameral legislature is
    a. Maine.
    b. Massachusetts.
    c. Indiana.
    d. Nebraska.

11. Which of the following state legislatures is MOST professionalized?
    a. New Hampshire
    b. North Dakota
    c. California
    d. Wyoming

12. What is the MOST dominant factor affecting the relationship between a state's governor and legislature?
    a. The salary structure of the governor and legislators.
    b. The level of professionalization of the state legislature.
    c. The amount of staff in the state legislature.
    d. The political party affiliation of the governor and the legislature.

13. The term-limitation movement has been largely pushed by
    a. the feminist movement.
    b. several national conservative organizations.
    c. liberal Democrats.
    d. a grass roots movement sweeping across the entire country.

14. What is the SINGLE most influential interest group in state politics?
    a. Lobbyists for the environmental movement
    b. Lobbyists for farmers
    c. Lobbyists for the public school teachers
    d. Lobbyists for civil liberties

15. What was the result of the curtailing of federal assistance to the states in the Reagan era?
    a. Lobbying at the state level increased dramatically.
    b. Lobbying at the federal level increased dramatically.
    c. There was no significant change in the level of lobbying activity at the state level.
    d. Lobbyists at the state level no longer had to register and disclose their employers.

16. Which of the following is an example of direct democracy?
    a. Term limits
    b. Initiative
    c. Line-item veto
    d. Professionalized legislature

17. Most of the revenue generated in states comes from
    a. "sin taxes" (taxes on alcohol and tobacco).
    b. taxes on corporations.
    c. taxes on motor fuels.
    d. sales taxes and individual income taxes.

18. During the early part of the twentieth century, what was the major source of state revenue?
    a. Property taxes
    b. Lotteries
    c. Gambling
    d. Corporate income taxes

19. What does the U.S. Constitution say about local governments in the U.S.?
    a. All local governments will have 3 branches, just like the federal and state governments.
    b. All local areas will be guaranteed a republican form of government.
    c. Nothing.
    d. All local areas will have the right to direct democracy, if the citizens choose to exercise it.

20. What is the most popular form of government at the local level?
    a. City commission
    b. Council-manager
    c. Mayor-council
    d. Town meetings

Essays

21. Discuss the nature of federalism from the beginning of the republic to the present time. How has the relationship between the federal government and the states evolved in U.S. history?
22. What are the three major types of federal assistance to state and local governments? How do they differ?
23. Compare the U.S. Constitution with state constitutions. Which has been more stable over time? Why?
24. Discuss the reforms that many state legislatures undertook in the 1960s. How successful have these efforts been in general? Explain.
25. What are the three typical governing structures at the local level? Be sure to list the strengths and weaknesses of each type.

CRITICAL THINKING EXERCISES

1. If possible, schedule a trip to your state capital and visit your state legislature (perhaps you can go with a group of your peers). Call in advance so you can witness the legislature while it is in session. Find out the size of your state legislature. Which political party controls the lower chamber, and which political party controls the upper chamber (outside of Nebraska, that is)? By what margins? Who represents you in your state legislature? If the legislature is in session, try to schedule a meeting with your own representative and/or senator.

2.   What kind of local government structure do you have in your home town or city? In order to compare the structure in your town or city with that of others similar in size, find out the current population in the place that you consider home. What kinds of structures exist in other cities or towns that are comparable in size?

3.   Write an essay entitled "Term Limits at the State and National Level." Are term limits at both levels a good idea or not? Are they constitutional in your opinion? Be sure to develop several justifications in support of your argument.

ANSWERS TO THE PRACTICE EXAM

1.	C	11.	C
2.	C	12.	D
3.	D	13.	B
4.	B	14.	C
5.	A	15.	A
6.	B	16.	B
7.	B	17.	D
8.	C	18.	A
9.	A	19.	C
10.	D	20.	C

21.   The nature of federalism has evolved dramatically in U.S. history. For approximately the first 140 years of the existence of the republic, the federal government provided very little aid to state and local governments (less than 1% of all state and local revenues as late as World War I). The relations between the national and subordinate levels of government were governed by the idea of dual federalism, which held that the national government was supreme in specific policy areas delineated in the Constitution, and the states were supreme in other areas of public policy. In other words, to a very large extent, the federal and state governments did not interact and work together to address societal problems. This tradition of separatism under dual federalism collapsed in the 1930s with the advent of the New Deal programs espoused by President Franklin D. Roosevelt. A new tradition in federalism evolved called fiscal federalism. Under fiscal federalism, the federal government has played an active role in providing financial assistance to the state and local governments. By 1980, the federal government provided for more than 30% of all state and local revenue. Since this time, however, the federal government's contribution to state and local revenues fell to less than 20% by 1990 due to the elimination of many federal aid programs by President Ronald Reagan. Nevertheless, the federal government remains one of the major sources of state and local revenues.

22.   There are three major types of federal assistance to state and local governments. The most common type since the 1930s is the categorical grant-in-aid. Categorical grants-in-aid are grants of money from the federal government to state and local governments for specific purposes such as highway construction. The recipients have to follow detailed federal rules that govern how the money can be spent. Another type that surfaced in the early 1970s is the block grant. Block grants are grants of money from the federal government to state and local governments for broad policy purposes, such as economic development, rather than for specific purposes as is the case with categorical grants. In 1972, Congress also initiated a third type of federal assistance: revenue sharing. This is a program that gives federal money to state and local governments with no restrictions on how it can be spent. This program, however, was ended in 1986.

23.   Similar to the federal constitution, state constitutions establish the basic rules of the political system. Yet state constitutions have been far less stable than the U.S. Constitution for two significant reasons. First, most state constitutions are much more detailed and specific than the federal constitution. This is clearly demonstrated in the length of the documents themselves. The U.S. Constitution, compared to the state documents, is very short and broad in its language. Such is not the case at the state level. The detail in the state constitutions makes them less flexible and more often in need of change. Secondly, state constitutions have changed far more

frequently than the federal constitution. The U.S. Constitution has only been amended 27 times since the birth of the nation. Most state constitutions have not been that stable. Approximately half of the state constitutions have been amended over 100 times. State constitutions change frequently because the rules make it easy for dissatisfied groups to pass constitutional amendments. In addition to this, most states have had several constitutions, whereas the federal government has only had two in U.S. history (the Articles of Confederation marked the first attempt at governing as an independent nation).

24. During the 1960s, many state legislatures undertook a series of reforms, collectively referred to as professionalization. In general, the reforms greatly strengthened their power. Up until the 1960s, most state governors exercised far more political power than did their legislatures. This changed in many states due largely to the reform efforts of Jesse Unruh in California. Member pay was increased and service in the legislature was made more attractive and affordable in those states that developed a more professionalized legislature. Staff resources and facilities were expanded, and this enabled many legislators to counter the governor's traditional advantages in expertise and staff. In many states, laws limiting the length of legislative sessions were eliminated. Reformers desired to make state legislatures more like the U.S. Congress. Determining the success of the reformers is a difficult task. Less professional legislatures are not necessarily less effective. Legislators in professionalized legislatures serve longer and understand more about how government works in general. They have more staff, more information at their disposal, and are better equipped to initiate policy making, which in turn means that they are less inclined to adopt the governor's preferences. Does this mean that legislators in professionalized legislatures are more effective at law making? Are laws passed in states like California, Massachusetts, Michigan, and New York better than in states with less professionalized legislatures such as New Hampshire, North Dakota, South Dakota, Utah, and Wyoming? While the benefits of professionalized legislatures are numerous, the general public gives them lower approval ratings than they do less professionalized legislatures. Regardless of professionalization, the partisanship of the governor and the legislature still dominates executive-legislative relations at the state level.

25. The three common governing structures at the local level are the mayor-council form, the city commission form, and the council-manager form of government. The most popular form is the mayor-council form, which can have either strong or weak mayors. If the governing structure provides for a strong mayor, he or she has the same kinds of executive powers exercised by the president and governors. In a weak mayor form, the mayor is essentially a figurehead, and the council performs all executive functions. Because of accountability, many people prefer having a strong mayor. In this manner, one person is truly held responsible for executive activity. The city commission form of government combines legislative and executive functions in one elected group. Commissioners make policy as a group, but each commissioner also heads a major department of government. One commissioner is named the mayor and presides over commission meetings. One problem is that elected officials do not always have the managerial skills to lead their departments in an effective manner. In the council-manager form of government, a city manager is hired by the elected city council to implement its policies. This form was created in large part to separate politics from administration. Yet it is not uncommon for city managers to become a powerful force in setting policies, even though this is technically the task of the city council.

SUMMARY

Spending has grown considerably since the birth of the republic, and the federal government now spends over $1.6 trillion every year. In fact, the growth in spending has been greater than the growth in revenues, resulting in an annual budget deficit in excess of $150 billion in recent years. The overall national debt is much greater than the budget deficit—over $5 trillion in 1995. Both Congress and the president are partially to blame for the debt problem. The American public, however, is also responsible because Congress and the president respond to the public's demand for more services and lower taxes every year the budget is assembled and debated.

OUTLINE

Opening Story: The Shut Down of the Federal Government in 1995 and 1996

In November 1995, the federal government shut down. On a typical day, 700,000 people visit the nation's national parks, 55,000 tourists visit monuments in Washington, D.C., 28,000 retirees apply for Social Security benefits, and 700 young men and women join the armed forces. At this time, however, they all found that the federal government was closed for business.

Why was the federal government shut down? This occurred because the Congress and President Clinton were unable to agree on a new budget for the federal government. By law, the president and Congress have until September 30 of each year to agree on a budget for the next fiscal year. Quite often, the Congress and the president fail to complete work by the September 30 deadline, but they keep the government open by passing short-term spending bills that keep programs in operation until a final agreement is reached. In 1995, however, President Clinton and the Republican majority in Congress were too far apart for any long-term agreement to be reached.

After a short-term spending bill expired in mid-November, the federal government lost its authority to spend money and it had to shut down for all non-essential services. A week later a new short-term spending bill was passed, but then the same pattern was repeated: a short-term spending bill expired, and parts of the federal government shut down again. The shutdown of the federal government in late 1995 and early 1996 illustrates a reality faced by all government officials: the programs that people would like the government to fund far exceed the government's resources.

Budgets, Deficit Spending, and the National Debt (p. 528)

The Growing Federal Budget (p. 529)

The Rise of Deficit Spending (p. 530)

The Exploding National Debt (p. 532)

The Consequences of an Exploding National Debt (p. 533)

Where Does Government Revenue Come From? (p. 534)

Government Revenue in Historical Perspective (p. 534)

Income and Payroll Taxes (p. 535)

Where Does Government Spending Go? (p. 538)

The Changing Nature of Government Spending (p. 538)

The Growth of Entitlement Programs (p. 539)

Limiting Entitlement Programs (p. 543)

What About Pork? (p. 544)

Why Do Budget Deficits Persist? (p. 546)

Congress and the President (p. 546)

The American Public (p. 546)

The Budgetary Process (p. 548)

The Budgetary Process from George Washington to Richard Nixon (p. 548)

Budgetary Reform in the 1970s (p. 549)

Budgetary Reform in the 1980s (p. 551)

Budgetary Reform in the 1990s (p. 553)

A Balanced Budget by 2002? (p. 553)

More Reforms? (p. 556)

Is the Budget Process Irrational? (p. 560)

Summary (p. 561)

Key Terms (p. 562)

Readings for Further Study (p. 562)

KEY TERMS, CONCEPTS, EVENTS, AND PEOPLE

Be able to identify and/or define each of the following and state its importance in a short paragraph.

Budget deficit (p. 529)

National debt (p. 529)

Balanced budget (p. 529)

Budget surplus (p. 529)

Social Security Act of 1935 (p. 535)

Progressive tax (p. 536)

Regressive tax (p. 537)

Entitlement programs (p. 539)

Cost-of-living adjustment (COLA) (p. 539)

Non-discretionary spending (p. 543)

Discretionary spending (p. 543)

Pork barrel (p. 544)

Corporate welfare (p. 544)

Budget and Accounting Act of 1921 (p. 549)

Office of Management and Budget (OMB) (p. 549)

Congressional Budget and Impoundment Control Act of 1974 (p. 549)

Congressional Budget Office (CBO) (p. 549)

Continuing resolutions (p. 550)

Line-item veto (p. 556)

Flat tax (p. 559)

Revenue neutral (p. 559)

LEARNING OBJECTIVES

After reading chapter 16, students should be able to:

1. Describe the growth of the federal budget and the national debt over the course of the nation's history, including the recent surge of budget deficits.
2. Discuss the positive and negative consequences of budget deficits and the growing national debt.
3. Describe the sources of federal government revenue, including how those sources changed over time—especially with the adoption of the Sixteenth Amendment and the passage of the Social Security Act of 1935.
4. Recognize the progressive and regressive natures of some taxes and discuss the contending arguments in the debate over which sort of tax is preferable.
5. Describe the programs on which the federal government spends money.
6. Identify the major entitlement programs and explain why Congress and the president find them so difficult to limit.
7. Define what pork-barrel spending is and defend the claim that it represents only a small fraction of total spending by the federal government.
8. Discuss the political problems that make it difficult for the federal government to balance its budget.
9. Describe the changes in the budget process over the nation's history and explain the current budget process.
10. Define what the line-item veto is, discuss the arguments for and against its adoption, and understand the version of the line item veto (enhanced recision) now exercised by the president.
11. Explain why it is difficult to develop a rational budgetary process and discuss why incremental budgeting simplifies the problem of developing an ideal budget.

PRACTICE EXAM

(Answers appear at the end of this chapter)

Multiple Choice

1. The first federal budget deficits occurred in the
   a. 1790s.
   b. 1830s.
   c. 1930s.
   d. 1980s.

2. What accounts for the rapid growth in federal spending in the last 60 years?
   a. America's role as a military superpower.
   b. The increase in the federal government's role in American life.
   c. Dwight David Eisenhower's New Deal programs.
   d. Both a and b.

3. Federal budget deficits have been common in the U.S. since
   a. the early 1920s.
   b. the early 1940s.
   c. the early 1960s.
   d. the early 1980s.

4. Between 1982 and 1993, the national debt
   a. remained constant.
   b. decreased.
   c. doubled.
   d. quadrupled.

5. What are the two most important sources of revenue for the federal government?
   a. Corporate income taxes and social insurance taxes.
   b. Personal income taxes and social insurance taxes.
   c. Personal income taxes and excise taxes.
   d. Personal income taxes and corporate income taxes.

6. What is the FICA tax?
   a. A federal tax on cigarettes.
   b. A federal tax on alcohol.
   c. Social security.
   d. A federal tax on highway users.

7. The federal tax code in the U.S. is
   a. regressive.
   b. misleading, because of loopholes.
   c. completely progressive.
   d. much higher than in most other industrialized countries.

8. What is the largest entitlement program?
   a. Social security
   b. Medicare
   c. Unemployment
   d. Food stamps

9. Which of the following statements is TRUE?
   a. Since 1940, overall spending on defense has decreased, and overall spending on human resources has increased.
   b. Since 1940, overall spending on defense and human resources has increased, but overall spending on the national debt interest has decreased.
   c. The percentage of the budget devoted to interest payments on the national debt doubled in the 1980s.
   d. Overall spending on defense has increased much faster than overall spending on human resources or interest payments on the national debt.

10. Spending on pork-barrel projects
    a. amounts to 25% of the federal budget.
    b. amounts to 15% of the federal budget.
    c. amounts to 5% of the federal budget.
    d. amounts to 1% of the federal budget.

11. Who is the main culprit for the federal budget deficit?
    a. Congress
    b. president
    c. American public
    d. Bureaucrats

12. The president was authorized to submit a single budget to Congress in
    a. 1860.
    b. 1892.
    c. 1921.
    d. 1967.

13. The Office of Management and Budget (OMB) was instituted in
    a. 1921.
    b. 1946.
    c. 1959.
    d. 1970.

14. Congress' version of the Office of Management and Budget (OMB) is the
    a. Congressional Management Office (CMO).
    b. Congressional Budget Office (CBO).
    c. Congressional Management and Budget Office (CMBO).
    d. Congressional Budget Committee (CBC).

15. Continuing resolutions
    a. keep the government running.
    b. have been used frequently since 1975.
    c. give Congress more time to debate the budget.
    d. All of the above.

16. What congressional attempt to reform the budgetary process occurred in the 1980s?
    a. Budget Enforcement Act (BEA)
    b. Gramm-Rudman
    c. Kennedy Initiative
    d. Dole Alternative

17. What was the impact of Gramm-Rudman?
    a. The federal budget deficit decreased by 50%.
    b. The federal budget deficit decreased by 10%.
    c. The federal budget deficit remained about the same.
    d. The federal budget deficit increased.

18. When is the beginning of the new federal fiscal year?
    a. October 1
    b. July 1
    c. April 1
    d. January 1

19. Who was the first president to request a line-item veto?
    a. Ulysses Grant
    b. Warren Harding
    c. Calvin Coolidge
    d. Richard Nixon

20. Balanced budget amendments
    a. would prevent future budget deficits.
    b. would force Congress to be fiscally responsible without wreaking havoc on the American economy and society.
    c. would balance the federal budget deficit immediately.
    d. are very popular with the American public.

Essays

21. What are the positive and negative consequences of a growing national debt? Explain.
22. At the present time, what are the major sources of revenue for the federal government? What are some other potential sources of revenue?
23. What are the four largest entitlement programs? What are the inherent difficulties in limiting the federal spending of these programs?
24. How did the budgetary process change from the beginning of the republic to the Nixon presidency?
25. What are some implications of a balanced budget amendment?

CRITICAL THINKING EXERCISES

1. You have just been elected president of the United States. The budget deficit stands at $150 billion, and the national debt is $5 trillion. In your first budget to Congress, what will you propose to help reduce these figures? How will you attempt to persuade both Congress and the American public that your budget is plausible and responsible?

2. Write an essay entitled, "Reforming the Budgetary Process of the Federal Government." Offer your own suggestions on how the process could be improved.

3. Do some research on the Social Security program. What are the current rules governing retirement? How does the program actually work? What are the long term forecasts for the program? What changes, if any, should be made to insure that the program is in tact when you reach retirement age?

ANSWERS TO THE PRACTICE EXAM

1.	A	11.	C
2.	D	12.	C
3.	C	13.	D
4.	D	14.	B
5.	B	15.	D
6.	C	16.	B
7.	B	17.	D
8.	A	18.	A
9.	C	19.	A
10.	D	20.	D

21.   All debt is not necessarily bad. Borrowing can be judicious if used for productive investment. Federal debt could actually be beneficial if the borrowed funds were utilized for improving the nation's economy. Yet debt is not always beneficial, either, and is highly problematic for at least two reasons. First, a rapidly growing debt may hurt economic growth. When the federal government borrows money, it competes with other borrowers, which raises interest rates. Higher interest rates can be detrimental to economic growth. Second, many fear that deficit spending goes less to finance productive investment and more to pay for current consumption. Borrowing to finance existing programs will do little to prepare the nation for the economic challenges of the future. Additionally, the cost of paying just the interest on the borrowed money is taking up a larger portion of the federal budget. Simply put, interest payments are funds that cannot be utilized for other important purposes.

22.   Currently, the major sources of revenue for the federal government are personal income taxes; social insurance taxes; corporate income taxes; estate, customs, and other taxes; as well as excise taxes. Billions of dollars are lost to the federal government because of exemptions in the tax code. The six most costly tax breaks include pension contributions and interest, the home mortgage deduction, employer paid health benefits, the social security exclusion, state and local income taxes, and charitable contributions. These, as well as many other smaller tax breaks, could increase federal revenues significantly. The tax exemptions, however, are very popular with the American public, and elected officials who try to repeal them may face defeat in their next campaign.

23.   The four largest entitlement programs are Social Security, Medicare, Deposit insurance, and Medicaid. Social security is by far the largest, and the federal government paid out approximately $340 billion in 1995 alone. Congress and the president have found it very difficult to cut these programs, both for political reasons (elected officials can pay a high price for reducing the benefits of their constituents), and because they are not able to control entitlement programs through the budgetary process (thus the term non-discretionary spending). Federal law stipulates that all citizens who meet the requirements of an entitlement program must receives its benefits. The only way Congress and the president can reduce an entitlement benefit is to rewrite the law that established it. But changing the rules of a program which gives benefits to people is a daunting task for a politician. Most avoid it for fear of political suicide. As a result, spending on entitlement programs is not likely to be curtailed.

24.   The federal budgetary process changed dramatically from George Washington to Richard Nixon. For most of the nineteenth century, the federal government followed a very simple budgetary process. Spending was low. Individual agencies in the executive branch submitted   their budgets directly to Congress. Until the mid-1860s, the House Ways and Means Committee and the Senate Finance Committee handled both tax and appropriations bills. The growth of the budget prompted the House and Senate to create a separate Appropriations Committee. As a result, one group of legislators had control over government revenues (Ways and Means in the House, and Finance in the Senate) and another group had control over spending (Appropriations in both chambers). This relatively simple process lasted until the post-World War I era when the national debt increased a great deal. Congress responded by passing the Budget and Accounting Act of 1921. The act authorized the president to submit a single budget to Congress for its inspection. The Bureau of the Budget (BOB) was created to assist the president in this endeavor. In 1970, President Nixon was responsible for reorganizing and renaming the BOB. It has been called the Office of Management and Budget (OMB) since then. Congress still has the right to review and change the president's budget.

25.   There are many implications of requiring the Congress and the president to balance the budget through a constitutional amendment. All proposals to date have not included any specifics as to how the budget would be balanced. Furthermore, a deficit as large as the one in the U.S. cannot be cut quickly without dire consequences on the economy and society. Because of this, most proposals have delayed the balancing of the budget to a point in time in the future. Finally, it is unlikely that a balanced budget amendment would prevent deficits in the first place. Many states with similar constitutional provisions still have debts.

SUMMARY

Three types of domestic policy are examined in this chapter: management of the economy, regulatory policy, and social welfare policy. In all three areas, the rules change as the needs and views of the American people and their elected representatives change. In domestic policy, as is true in all areas of government, changes in the rules cause some groups to gain and others to lose. An ongoing question in American politics, from the early days of the republic to the present, is the following: to what extent should the federal government intervene in the lives of people?

OUTLINE

Opening Story: Changing Attitudes Toward the Role of the Federal Government in the Lives of the American People

In his 1964 State of the Union address, President Lyndon Johnson announced his War on Poverty, and his intention to create a Great Society. Over the course of the 1960s, first under President Johnson and then under his Republican successor Richard Nixon, Congress passed legislation creating an array of programs that increased the federal government's role in domestic policy in the U.S.

Three decades later, much of the enthusiasm for an activist federal role in domestic policy had vanished. Republicans were especially critical of federal intervention in the private sector to address societal problems. Yet Republicans were not alone in their criticism of the Great Society programs. Many of Lyndon Johnson's fellow Democrats were reluctant to defend his vision of a federal government with expansive responsibilities in domestic policy. Indeed, in his 1996 State of the Union speech, President Bill Clinton declared that "the era of big government is over."

The changing attitudes toward the merits of the War on Poverty and the Great Society programs illustrate how conflict regarding the proper role of the federal government in domestic policy is omnipresent. As the views of Congress and the president toward the proper role of the federal government change, the rules of domestic policy change to either limit or expand the federal government's ability to intervene directly in domestic concerns.

Managing the Economy (p. 564)

From Government Restraint to Government Intervention (p. 565)

Managing the Economy by Taxing and Spending (p. 566)

Managing the Economy by Controlling the Money Supply (p. 567)

Can the Government Manage the Economy? (p. 569)

The Current Status of Economic Stewardship (p. 570)

Regulating Business (p. 574)

Basic Concepts and Categories (p. 575)

The Objectives of Economic Regulation (p. 575)

The Evolution of Economic Regulation (p. 576)

Social Regulation (p. 579)

Protecting Worker Safety and Health (p. 579)

Protecting the Environment (p. 581)

Promoting Social Welfare (p. 586)

Basic Concepts and Categories (p. 586)

The Evolution of Social Welfare Policy (p. 587)

The Current Status of Social Welfare Policy (p. 593)

The Future of Social Welfare Policy (p. 595)

Summary (p. 600)

Key Terms (p. 601)

Readings for Further Study (p. 601)

KEY TERMS, CONCEPTS, EVENTS, AND PEOPLE

Be able to identify and/or define each of the following and state its importance in a short paragraph.

Laissez faire (p. 565)

Fiscal policy (p. 566)

Gross domestic product (GDP) (p. 566)

Keynesian economics (p. 567)

Monetary theory (p. 567)

Federal Reserve System (p. 568)

Lucas critique (p. 569)

Supply-side economics (p. 573)

Industrial policy (p. 574)

Regulatory policy (p. 574)

Economic regulation (p. 575)

Social regulation (p. 575)

Environmental impact statement (p. 582)

Aid to Families with Dependent Children (AFDC) (p. 586)

Social welfare policy (p. 586)

Social insurance (p. 586)

Public assistance (p. 586)

Means test (p. 586)

Food Stamp program (p. 591)

Medicare (p. 592)

Medicaid (p. 592)

LEARNING OBJECTIVES

After reading chapter 17, students should be able to:

1. Sketch out the growth of the federal government's role in managing the economy.
2. Describe Keynesian economic theory and explain how the budget can be used as a fiscal policy tool.
3. Describe monetary theory, sketch out the organization of the Federal Reserve System, and explain how the Fed can influence the course of the economy.
4. Explain the conflicts surrounding the changing distribution of income and wealth in the United States, supply-side economics, and industrial policy.
5. Discuss the goals and evolution of economic regulation, from the beginning of economic regulation in the 1880s to the deregulation trend of the 1970s and 1980s.
6. Outline the range of social regulation policies and discuss the history of OSHA, including the controversies surrounding it in the 1980s and 1990s.
7. Describe the development of regulatory policies to protect the environment.
8. Discuss current conflicts about the proper regulatory course for future environmental protection efforts.
9. Describe the range of current social welfare policies and explain different ways in which they may be classified.
10. Sketch out the evolution of social welfare programs from the 1800s to the 1990s.
11. Assess the current status and success of social welfare policies.
12. Analyze the controversies surrounding the future directions of social security, welfare, and health policy.

PRACTICE EXAM

(Answers appear at the end of this chapter)

Multiple Choice

1. Who was the last president associated with laissez faire economic policies?
   a. Calvin Coolidge
   b. Herbert Hoover
   c. Franklin Roosevelt
   d. Dwight Eisenhower

2. The unemployment rate during the Great Depression was _____%.
   a. 5
   b. 15
   c. 25
   d. 50

3. Franklin Roosevelt's decision to use fiscal policy to combat the Great Depression was inspired by the work of
   a. John Maynard Keynes.
   b. Milton Friedman.
   c. Karl Marx.
   d. Alan Greenspan.

4. What independent regulatory commission was established by Congress in 1913 to act as a powerful central bank that could stabilize the nation's money supply?
   a. Internal Revenue Service
   b. Federal Reserve System
   c. Bank of America
   d. Congressional Budget Office

5. _____ was reappointed by President Bill Clinton in 1995 to be chair of the Federal Reserve System.
   a. Robert Reich
   b. Milton Friedman
   c. Lloyd Bentsen
   d. Alan Greenspan

6. The top 20% of U.S. households (those with a net worth of $180,000 or more) control more than _____% of the country's wealth.
   a. 20
   b. 40
   c. 60
   d. 80

7. Which ONE of the following is NOT supported by theorists espousing supply-side economics?
   a. Tax cuts for the wealthiest Americans
   b. Decrease in government spending
   c. Decrease in government regulation
   d. Tax increases for the wealthiest Americans

8. What has been the most recent phase of economic regulation?
   a. Deregulation.
   b. The government's role in regulating the economy has expanded tremendously.
   c. The government has only recently established a role for itself in regulating the economy.
   d. The government has allowed the private sector to regulate itself completely.

9. Before the mid-1960s,
   a. the federal government focused on cleaning up hazardous waste sites in environmental policy.
   b. the federal government focused on cleaning up air pollution in environmental policy.
   c. the federal government focused on land conservation in environmental policy.
   d. the federal government focused on cleaning up water pollution in environmental policy.

10. Which of the following is NOT a public assistance program?
    a. Medicaid
    b. Food Stamps
    c. Social Security
    d. AFDC

11. For the first half of our nation's history,
    a. poverty was addressed at the federal level.
    b. the poor were often blamed for their own situation.
    c. public assistance was viewed as a local responsibility.
    d. Both b + c

12. _____ introduced the first major wave of social welfare policies in the U.S.
    a. The Social Security Act of 1935
    b. The Great Society
    c. The War on Poverty
    d. The Economic Opportunity Act of 1955

13. Which of the following were created during President Lyndon Johnson's War on Poverty?
    a. Head Start
    b. Food Stamp program
    c. Medicare
    d. All of the above

14. What is the largest social insurance program in the U.S.?
    a. AFDC
    b. Social Security
    c. Medicare
    d. Medicaid

15. The infant mortality rate in the U.S. has _____ over the past three decades.
    a. increased dramatically
    b. increased slightly
    c. remained constant
    d. decreased

16. During the contentious congressional debates of 1995,
    a. the Republicans insisted that Social Security benefits must be reduced for a majority of Americans.
    b. the Democrats insisted that Social Security benefits must be reduced for a majority of Americans.
    c. the Republicans insisted that the Social Security program must be eliminated by the federal government.
    d. both Democrats and Republicans agreed that the Social Security program would not be altered.

17. An overwhelming majority of Americans
    a. is satisfied with the current social welfare system.
    b. endorses the idea that the federal government should provide a social safety net of welfare programs for the poor.
    c. believes that AFDC benefits should be at least doubled for most recipients.
    d. believes that a national health care system would be an improvement over the status quo.

18. What are the central issues in health care policy?
    a. Cost and access
    b. Cost and political ideology
    c. Access and influence
    d. Access and individualism

19. At any given time, about _____% of Americans have no health insurance.
    a. 2
    b. 10
    c. 17
    d. 43

20. _____ pays more per capita for medical care than any other major industrial nation.
    a. Canada
    b. Great Britain
    c. The United States
    d. Japan

Essays

21.   How does the Federal Reserve System control the money supply? Explain.
22.   How does social regulation differ from economic regulation? Explain.
23.   Besides enhancing the public interest at a given cost, what four factors shape the course of the political debate over environmental regulations? Explain.
24.   Social welfare programs can be classified according to the strategy they use to improve the recipients' quality of life. What are they and how do they differ?
25.   What two important questions lie at the core of the debate regarding the future of Social Security? Explain.

CRITICAL THINKING EXERCISES

1.   Devise your own plan for environmental protection in the U.S. How much of a role should the federal government have in this objective?
2.   After investigating Lyndon Johnson's presidency, what is your assessment of his objective of creating a "Great Society?" In your response, be sure to include your own views on the proper role of the federal government in the private sector.
3.   Research the pros and cons of a national health care system. Would this be plausible in the U.S.? Why or why not?

ANSWERS TO THE PRACTICE EXAM

1.	B	11.	D
2.	C	12.	A
3.	A	13.	D
4.	B	14.	B
5.	D	15.	D
6.	D	16.	D
7.	D	17.	B
8.	A	18.	A
9.	C	19.	C
10.	C	20.	C

21.   The Federal Reserve System controls the money supply that lies at the core of monetary theory in two ways. First, it sets the discount rate. The discount rate is the interest rate that the Fed charges its member banks when it lends them money. If the Fed wishes to reduce the money supply and slow down the economy, it can raise the discount rate, thus making it more expensive to borrow money. Similarly, if it wishes to increase the money supply, it can lower the discount rate. Second, the other primary method the Fed has to effect the money supply is the buying and selling of treasuries, or government IOUs. When the Fed wishes to change the amount of money in circulation, it does not simply turn on or off the presses that print money. Instead, the Fed buys or

sells treasuries. When the Fed sells treasuries, it takes money out of circulation and leaves the purchaser with a bond—a piece of paper promising to repay the purchaser the principal plus interest over a set period of time. When the Fed buys treasuries, it redeems bonds already in circulation and thereby puts more money into circulation.

22.   Social regulation differs from economic regulation in two important ways. First, whereas economic regulations usually are industry-specific, social regulations tend to cut across industries. Government regulations on work and product safety, the environment, and equal opportunity are examples of social regulation that apply to all industries. Second, social regulations are usually grounded in very specific, technical legislation rather than vague guidelines that require federal agencies to protect the public interest.

23.   Besides enhancing the public interest at a given cost, four other factors shape the course of political debate over environmental regulations. First, environmental regulations tend to produce diffuse benefits spread across society while imposing focused costs that affect relatively few businesses or individuals. The benefits tend to be spread out across the entire country, and many people do not notice them. In contrast, the affected businesses will be acutely aware of the costs of regulation. Second, the benefits of some environmental regulations are difficult to measure, but the costs are not. Third, measuring the magnitude of environmental problems can be difficult. Fourth, protecting the environment becomes increasingly costly as the standards of environmental quality rise.

24.   One strategy is alleviate, and it encompasses programs that attempt to soften, or alleviate, the hardships of poverty. Most public assistance programs are alleviative. A second strategy is preventative, and it encompasses programs that require individuals to take actions today (making contributions, for example, to a social insurance program) to prevent themselves from falling into poverty later in life. A third strategy is curative, and it encompasses programs such as Head Start and job training that seek to cure poverty by giving the poor the skills they need to lift themselves out of poverty.

25.   Two important questions lie at the core of the debate regarding the future of the Social Security program. First, on whom should the federal government spend its money? The federal government spends nearly eleven times more per capita on the elderly than on the young. Should the federal government, therefore, continue to spend so heavily on Social Security for the elderly when far more children than senior citizens live in poverty. Second, is Social Security headed for insolvency? The flaw with this "pay-as-you-go" system is that over the years the ratio of workers paying taxes to retirees drawing benefits has fallen. In 1950, there were fifteen workers for every retiree; in 1990, there were only five. Experts predict by 2030, there will be fewer than three. If this trend continues unchanged, some time in the next twenty years the annual cost of Social Security will exceed the revenue from payroll taxes, and once the surpluses that have been built up over the years are exhausted, Social Security will become insolvent.

Chapter *18* Foreign Policy

SUMMARY

Until the attack on Pearl Harbor in 1941, policy makers in the United States spent most of the nation's history avoiding alliances with other countries. After World War II, however, the U.S. became a superpower and ended approximately 150 years of isolationism. The new focus of U.S. foreign policy became known as containment, and it guided America's foreign policy for almost half a century. With the demise of the Soviet Union and the triumph of containment in recent years, foreign policy officials in the U.S. struggle to define America's role in the world in the 1990s and beyond.

OUTLINE

Opening Story: The Peacekeeping Mission in Bosnia

In 1992, Croats, Muslims, and Serbs began to wage a war for control of Bosnia, a republic in the former Yugoslavia. The war raged on and off for three years, and it is estimated that 250,000 people were killed. Many analysts feared that the fighting in Bosnia might spread to other parts of Europe, thereby jeopardizing the political stability that the U.S. had sought for nearly fifty years to preserve. By the end of 1995, at the urging of U.S. officials, a peace treaty was signed in Dayton, Ohio. To give peace a chance to take root, President Clinton and America's European allies agreed to send more than 60,000 peacekeeping troops to Bosnia, including 20,000 Americans.

The peacekeeping mission in Bosnia illustrates that the U.S. has interests beyond its borders. Because world events can have a dramatic effect on U.S. interests, officials in the federal government must succeed in formulating judicious policies in the area of foreign affairs.

A Brief History of U.S. Foreign Policy (p. 604)

The Era of Isolationism (p. 604)

The Era of Globalism (p. 607)

After the Cold War (p. 610)

Foreign Policy Versus Domestic Policy (p. 611)

The Constitution and Foreign Policy (p. 612)

The President's Inherent Advantages (p. 612)

Precedent (p. 613)

Supreme Court Rulings (p. 613)

The Behavior of Congress (p. 615)

Who Makes U.S. Foreign Policy? (p. 617)

The White House (p. 618)

The Foreign Policy Bureaucracy (p. 618)

Congress (p. 624)

The Public (p. 625)

Challenges to the United States in the Post-Cold War Era (p. 627)

Economic and Budgetary Constraints (p. 627)

A Changing Foreign Policy Agenda (p. 629)

Unilateralism Versus Multilateralism (p. 631)

Summary (p. 634)

Key Terms (p. 635)

Readings for Further Study (p. 635)

KEY TERMS, CONCEPTS, EVENTS, AND PEOPLE

Be able to identify and/or define each of the following and state its importance in a short paragraph.

Isolationism (p. 604)

Monroe Doctrine (p. 605)

Globalism (p. 607)

Truman Doctrine (p. 607)

Marshall Plan (p. 607)

Containment (p. 608)

Cold War (p. 608)

North Atlantic Treaty Organization (NATO) (p. 608)

Third World (p. 608)

Detente (p. 610)

Enlargement (p. 611)

Neo-isolationism (p. 611)

National interest (p. 611)

Two presidencies (p. 612)

Executive agreements (p. 615)

Free trade (p. 629)

General Agreement on Tariffs and Trade (GATT) (p. 629)

Intermistic issues (p. 630)

Unilateralism (p. 631)

Multilateralism (p. 631)

World Trade Organization (WTO) (p. 632)

Sovereignty (p. 632)

LEARNING OBJECTIVES

After reading chapter 18, students should be able to:

1. Explain the basic thrust of American foreign policy during the isolationist era (1789-1941)
2. Discuss how containment was the fundamental foreign policy of the United States during the era of globalism (1941-1989).
3. Explain why the national consensus in favor of a policy of global containment crumbled in Vietnam.
4. Explain how the collapse of the Soviet Union affected U.S. foreign policy.
5. Define the concept of the national interest and assess the claim that a consensus exists among the American people about America's role in the world.
6. Explain the concept of the two presidencies and discuss why presidents tend to have greater influence over foreign policy than domestic policy.
7. Explain why Congress is often at a disadvantage relative to the president when it comes to foreign policy.
8. Discuss the respective roles of the White House, the foreign policy bureaucracy, Congress, and the public in the making of foreign policy.
9. Discuss the work of the National Security Council (NSC) and its staff.
10. Discuss the tasks performed by the foreign policy bureaucracy and analyze the work of the State Department, the Defense Department, and the Intelligence Community.
11. Discuss the tools that members of Congress use to influence U.S. foreign policy.
12. Discuss the extent to which the American public follows foreign affairs and assess the degree of influence the American public has on U.S. foreign policy.
13. Describe the economic and budgetary constraints facing the federal government and discuss the consequences these constraints have for U.S. foreign policy in the post-Cold War era.
14. Discuss how the nature of the issues on the U.S. foreign policy agenda has changed since the collapse of the Soviet Union and explain why these changes pose great challenges for the president.
15. Explain why the ability of the United States to act unilaterally in foreign policy is declining and discuss the problems that the need for multilateralism will present to government officials.

PRACTICE EXAM

(Answers appear at the end of this chapter)

Multiple Choice

1. U.S. diplomacy between 1789-1941 is referred to as
   a. the Washingtonian era.
   b. the Jeffersonian era.
   c. the isolationist era.
   d. the globalist era.

2. U.S. diplomacy between 1942-1989 is referred to as
   a. the Truman era.
   b. the New Frontier.
   c. the isolationist era.
   d. the globalist era.

3. The Clinton administration proposed to replace the policy of containment with the policy of
   a. the Clinton Doctrine.
   b. enlargement.
   c. enrichment.
   d. neo-isolationism.

4. In 1823, which president warned Europe that the Americas were "henceforth not to be considered as subjects for future colonization."
   a. Thomas Jefferson
   b. James Madison
   c. James Monroe
   d. John Quincy Adams

5. After World War I, the U.S. returned to its tradition of
    a. isolationism.
    b. globalism.
    c. containment.
    d. selective incorporation.

6. The Marshall Plan helped
    a. Western European countries rebuild their economies after World War I.
    b. Western European countries rebuild their economies after World War II.
    c. Western European countries rebuild their militaries after World War I.
    d. Western European countries rebuild their militaries after World War II.

7. When was the policy of containment first tested?
    a. Cuban Missile Crisis
    b. Vietnam War
    c. Korean War
    d. World War II

8. In all, how many Americans died in the Vietnam War?
    a. More than 12,000
    b. More than 32,000
    c. More than 47,000
    d. More than 58,000

9. The Berlin Wall fell in
    a. 1983.
    b. 1985.
    c. 1989.
    d. 1991.

10. Which president established the policy of detente?
    a. Lyndon Johnson
    b. Richard Nixon
    c. Gerald Ford
    d. Jimmy Carter

11. Which of the following DOES NOT explain why presidents typically have more say in foreign policy than domestic policy?
    a. A literal reading of the Constitution.
    b. Precedents established by earlier presidents.
    c. Rulings of the Supreme Court.
    d. Actions of Congress.

12. Which of the following powers WAS NOT granted to the president under the Constitution?
    a. Commander in chief of the army and navy of the U.S.
    b. Power to appoint ambassadors
    c. Power to make treaties
    d. Power to declare war

13. In which case did the Supreme Court justices rule that executive agreements are as binding as treaties?
    a. *U.S. v. Nixon*
    b. *U.S. v. Curtiss-Wright Export Corporation*
    c. *U.S. v. Belmont*
    d. *U.S. v. Truman*

14. Congress has formally declared war four times in U.S. history. Which of the following summaries is correct?
    a. War of 1812, Spanish-American War, World War I, and World War II.
    b. American Revolution, Civil War, World War I, and World War II.
    c. War of 1812, Civil War, World War I, and World War II.
    d. World War I, World War II, Korean War, and Vietnam War.

15. Who is the single most important actor in foreign policy?
    a. National Security Advisor
    b. Secretary of State
    c. Secretary of Defense
    d. President

16. The U.S. foreign service has traditionally been
    a. diverse.
    b. representative of the American public.
    c. elite.
    d. dominated by minorities.

17. What is the world's largest office building?
    a. White House
    b. Pentagon
    c. Sears Tower
    d. U.S. Capitol

18. Who is the head of the intelligence community?
    a. Secretary of State
    b. National Security Advisor
    c. Director of Central Intelligence Agency
    d. Director of Federal Bureau of Investigation

19. The world's largest debtor nation is
    a. Brazil.
    b. Mexico.
    c. Russia.
    d. the United States.

20. Which of the following poses the greatest challenge for U.S. policy makers?
    a. Domestic issues
    b. Foreign issues
    c. Intermistic issues
    d. All of the above.

Essays

21. Describe U.S. foreign policy in the post-Cold War period.
22. What is the two presidencies thesis? Where does a president get his or her strength in foreign policy matters? Explain.
23. Who are the main players that help to shape U.S. foreign policy? Explain.
24. What are some of the economic and budgetary constraints on policy making in the U.S.?
25. What is multilateralism, and why is it important in U.S. foreign policy?

CRITICAL THINKING EXERCISES

1. Try to improve your knowledge of world geography. Divide the globe into its seven continents (Africa, Antarctica, Asia, Australia, Europe, North America, and South America) and learn where the nations of the world are located. (This may not be a bad idea for U.S. geography either!)
2. Make a list of nations in the Northern hemisphere, and a list of nations in the Southern hemisphere. What similarities and/or differences exist among them?
3. Using a reference librarian for assistance, develop a list of the top ten most populous nations. In addition to this, find out a reliable estimate of the world's current population. What problems are posed by the world's growing population? How can these issues be resolved?

ANSWERS TO THE PRACTICE EXAM

1.	C	11.	A
2.	D	12.	D
3.	B	13.	C
4.	C	14.	A
5.	A	15.	D
6.	B	16.	C
7.	C	17.	B
8.	D	18.	C
9.	C	19.	D
10.	B	20.	C

21. Since the demise of the former Soviet Union, the U.S. has had a great deal of freedom to maneuver in world politics. As a result, in the post-Cold War era, the U.S. has intervened in many areas of the world (e.g., Panama, Persian Gulf, Somalia, and Haiti). Many have called for a new U.S. foreign policy, but a consensus on the rules has not been achieved. The Clinton administration has proposed to replace the policy of containment with one of enlargement, though by no means has this foreign policy approach garnered widespread approval. Some analysts argue that the U.S. should continue defining its interests in global terms, while others believe that the U.S. should focus more on domestic internal matters. Regardless of outcomes, the construction of a new U.S. foreign policy will be a complex process.

22. According to the two presidencies thesis, presidents have much greater influence over foreign policy matters than domestic policy matters. The presidents strength in foreign policy largely stems from four sources. First, the president has inherent advantages in foreign policy making. Congress is much more willing to challenge the content of domestic policy than foreign policy. The president has distinct advantages in terms of knowledge and information. The inherent advantages are greatest in a crisis situation, where Congress has little choice but to follow the president's lead. A second source of presidential strength in foreign affairs deals with the precedents established by earlier presidents. Presidents frequently cite precedents set by their predecessors to justify foreign policy intervention. A third source is the Supreme Court, and a series of its rulings which have expanded the president's authority in foreign affairs. The Court has ruled, for example, that the president's foreign policy powers go beyond what is mentioned in the Constitution, and that executive agreements are as binding as treaties. Fourth, the president's great strength in foreign policy stems from the actual behavior of members of Congress. Without widespread agreement among the members of the Congress, it is unable to act, especially in a period of crisis. As a result, many members of Congress believe that a successful foreign policy can only evolve through strong presidential leadership.

23. There are several players that help to shape the content of U.S. foreign policy. The president is the single most important actor. He or she receives advice and information from the National Security Council, the Central Intelligence Agency, and the Joint Chiefs of Staff. While presidents have a great deal of influence in this area, other players wield influence as well. The agencies of the foreign policy bureaucracy (State Department, Defense Department, intelligence community, and several other federal agencies) can help to shape foreign policy as well. The Constitution gives Congress considerable powers in foreign policy. Depending on the era, the extent of congressional influence over foreign policy has varied tremendously. The American public can also affect the direction of U.S. foreign policy. This can be accomplished in two significant ways: by becoming members of interest groups, and by voting for presidential candidates who share their preferences in foreign affairs.

24. In 1992, the U.S. became the world's largest debtor nation. Although the U.S. economy is still the largest in the world, it lags behind many of its economic competitors in many areas. As a result, there are several economic and budgetary constraints on U.S. foreign policy. New programs that require a great deal of spending are not likely to be approved, regardless of their necessity. Existing programs may suffer large cuts or be eliminated altogether. The impact of budgetary constraints has already been witnessed in the last decade. Spending for foreign aid has decreased by approximately 20% between 1990 and 1996. A program similar to the Marshall Plan is difficult to envision in our world today. The economic problems facing the U.S. are also likely to make Americans a bit more isolationist. Free trade is a good example. When unemployment increased in the 1980s and 1990s, public support for free trade decreased. The North American Free Trade Agreement (NAFTA) was almost defeated in 1993. If the American economy had been healthier, the NAFTA debate would not have been nearly as contentious as it was.

25. Multilateralism is an approach to foreign policy in which three or more countries cooperate with one another for the purpose of solving common problems. It is very important in U.S. foreign policy, because many issues cannot be resolved satisfactorily without mutual cooperation. Global warming is a good example. The U.S. is the single largest producer of heat-trapping gases responsible for global warming. A solution to this problem,

however, cannot be achieved by U.S. policy alone. Because the world is complex with vexatious problems to solve, the U.S. must rely on multilateral solutions for multilateral problems. While the U.S. has traditionally dominated multilateral institutions, its ability to continue doing so is diminishing. The Europeans and Japanese, in particular, can utilize their economic wealth to influence decision making in multilateral institutions. They are also less likely to defer to U.S. leadership, as they no longer need the U.S. to protect them militarily against the Soviet Union.